Frances Minturn Howard

BEACON HILL

Hub of the Universe

BEACON HILL
Hub of the Universe

by **Frances Minturn Howard**

Illustrated by **Mark Kelley**
Foreword by **David McCord**

Published MCMLXXVII by
YANKEE, INC.
Dublin, New Hampshire

This Book Has Been Prepared by the Staff of Yankee, Inc.
Deborah Stone, Editor
Ray Maher, Designer

FIRST EDITION

Printed in the United States of America

Library of Congress Catalog Card No. 77-80113
ISBN 0-911658-77-7

to my long-suffering partner in adventure and misadventure, Thomas Clark Howard

CONTENTS

FOREWORD

More than forty years ago, when I was down in Maine learning — or trying to learn — how to paint watercolors, I occasionally ate my supper in the small public dining room of a small private house. The waiter in his clean white apron was the young son of the lady who did the cooking and collected the dollar bill. A lobsterman by day, answering to the solemn name of Waldo, he usually opened (and frequently closed) the conversation between himself and the diner. One evening he presented me with an excellent bread pudding for dessert, and then withdrew at a respectful distance to watch me eat it. After adding a little cream and sugar to the dish, I slowly picked up my spoon. This was too much for Waldo, who said (carefully shrouding in Maine fog the final "r"): "Don't you want some butter?" I said "No, thank you, Waldo." A brief silence; and then he tried once more, with a slippery little sadness in his voice: "My grandfather always said, 'A good bread puddin' deserves some butter, and a bad one needs it'."

So it is, I think, with books and forewords. The part of Waldo, if well played by the publisher, should be productive; and the resulting pat of unsweetened typographical butter entice the buyer/reader into the secure belief that he or she will be repaid in the pages just beyond. And even — to shift the obliging metaphor — if its creator beats around a bush no bigger than a geranium, as this one is doing, he must try to suggest, without seeming to do so, the very *tone* of the book itself: serious, light-hearted, didactic, or whatever.

I believe that a foreword should be nothing more than an impulsive act of pure enthusiasm: I like this book so much that I want to tell people about it. All of us at times do this verbally — What? You *don't* know *The Outermost House? The Crock of Gold? The Small Years?*

Well, let me tell you why you should read this delightful book about Beacon Hill in Boston. First of all, as Melville says in *Moby Dick,* "It is not down in any map; true places never are." Physically it is; but the inhabitants, no. How Frances Howard manages to get them down where you can see them is her secret. This is not a book compiled out of books, but a living book of live observations. A book of grace and wit, and gentle, fine reporting. Though it is, and was designed to be, light-hearted, the author's determination to understand, appreciate, and *not* undervalue is something the social historian should make note of.

A deft and deftly controlled piece of writing, so it seems to me. I myself would begin at the back of this book, to be greeted there by Abigail, who reads dictionaries in bed for amusement. This will prepare you grandly to enter "the great superbly furnished house, floor-to-ceiling tapestried and riddled with imposing marble statuary... as unheated as a storage vault.... No, Boston is never dull," says Frances Howard. "It is not a place, like New York, where pleasure is a duty; but you would have to go a long way to find people more adept at turning duty into pleasure."

Frances Howard is a New Yorker. I was born in Manhattan. I see Beacon Hill not as a native. I see it, lifting some words from F.L. Lucas, "as above the long aridity of the Sahara stands up the range of Atlas." Frances Howard brings it all wonderfully into focus. No one else I know of has done this in detail before her. Certainly not with such charm and such wit.

David McCord

BEACON HILL

Hub of the Universe

Precepts for survival on Beacon Hill

When I first came to Boston I was dogged by a series of haunting sayings — tag ends of sentences which lodged disturbingly in my mind. The remark of our hostess' husband, for example, who politely saw us out one day after tea. As we said goodbye, I happened to comment on an interesting old painting — a Primitive, really — I had seen upstairs.

"My wife's mother was a Primitive," our host observed, meditatively.

And out we floated into the dark.

Another provocative comment came from an elderly neighbor, describing the husband of a friend. "*Was* he eccentric? He had toes sewed in his socks."

Eccentricities are usually, however, not called so in Boston; they are merely habits, stoutly defended.

"But why *shouldn't* she have herself listed in the telephone book in the name of a tree? All her *friends* know what tree to call."

There were other phrases like, "She lives on the Wrong Side of the Hill."

The Wrong Side — obviously not the place to be, but what penalties were attached? Where was the fine dividing line drawn?

There was, one day, a great display of shiny, red fire engines in front of a certain house on Chestnut Street.

"Oh," said a friend I was walking with, without any special interest, "I imagine it's just Letitia Allen's Annual Fire."

"Does she have a fire every year?"

"*Practically* every year. She missed last."

Buying an old house on Beacon Hill is equivalent, immediately, to a new education. You learn things from your neighbors, your in-laws, the policemen, the fire department — practically everyone is willing to instruct you. The janitors on Beacon Hill who come to take out your ash barrels biweekly and polish your brass doorknobs are reticent, courteous men who will not force their information on you; but they have it. Our first was a light colored cheerful fellow who wore a black beret dashingly on the side of his head; it took me some time to discover that he also spoke fluent Greek.

Mr. O'Malley, our first Hill policeman, was a liberal source of information in himself. If you met him, walking up The Hill in the morning, you could kiss goodbye to at least a half hour of your day. But it was worth it. Mr. O'Malley was a living encyclopedia; he was familiar with every family on Beacon Hill — where they lived and what their reputation. He was courteous with strangers; but I think he bristled a little, like a faithful dog, at the sight of one.

Mr. O'Malley had his own way of checking up on things. He did not barge in; he infiltrated. I was lying out in a long chair in our little back garden one fine spring day, reading, when finding myself suddenly in the shade, I looked up to see the not inconsiderable bulk of Mr. O'Malley outlined against the sun. The passageway door to the street had been left ajar, and Mr. O'Malley had come in by it. He was, he explained (for Mr. O'Malley never did anything out of vulgar curiosity; he always had a reason) "taking a look around for some police horses."

"Horses?" I said vaguely. "Oh, I don't think we could get any in here; the passageway is too narrow."

I thus revealed my ignorance. Mr. O'Malley meant, he explained, those wooden sawhorses placed in front of houses to reserve space for some emergency.

Our neighbors, an attractive young couple who had turned to and painted the front hall of their house a pale apple-green, were even more startled when Mr. O'Malley suddenly popped up beside them in their

Moving about under a flapping cloud of Mrs. C's skivvies, visitors felt distinctly ill at ease.

walnut-paneled library. They had been lounging there, exhausted, over a revivifying can of beer. (Again, the front door had been left open, to air out the smell of paint.)

"Well," said Mr. O'Malley, looking around at the walnut paneling of the library, "thank God you didn't paint *this,* anyway."

I made a most unfortunate social error early in my acquaintance with Mr. O'Malley; I gave a largish party and didn't invite him. But Mr. O'Malley was a big man, and he forgave me. He knew it was not ill will on my part, but simply ignorance. He came anyway.

His excuse for appearing was a large City Directory which he had promised one of my guests, the literary editor of a book review section of the newspaper; naturally, it had to be delivered there and then. Mr. O'Malley was introduced to the guest of honor, an author in whose works, it seemed, he took an interest; he then departed. I was not so inept again.

One of the first things that strikes a stranger in Boston about Beacon Hill is the odd times plumbing is done. To see a bathtub sitting out in the street at seven in the morning is a not uncommon sight. The fact is, all the old houses on Beacon Hill are so full of Violations that it is merely a question of whether an inspector wishes to clap one on you or not. Fire escapes wander crazily from one contiguous house to another. Retaining walls, common to two houses but the sole property of neither, are a fruitful source of guerilla combat. It is common knowledge that all improvements are noted with a jealous eye by Big Brother, the Tax Collector, and this is why you will see new bathtubs sitting outside on the curb before breakfast, to be rushed inside and installed before any inspectors are stirring.

I spent my first two years in Boston freezing to death. New York is a steam-heated place; Boston is not. I used to sit, on those rare occasions when we were invited out to dinner, trying not to hug my bare shoulders and speculating wildly on what kind of undergarments the other guests could be wearing that enabled them to sit, apparently, in comfort.

Certain people, I felt, carried this to extremes. At one of my first Reading Club afternoons I was astonished to see everybody, the moment we were let in the door by the uniformed maid, rush to a large pile of old sweaters, coats, and army blankets laid out helter-skelter on a handsome carved chair in the hall, and hastily climb into them. While I was still wondering at this, I began to shiver uncontrollably. The great superbly furnished house, floor-to-ceiling tapestried and riddled with imposing marble statuary, was as unheated as a storage vault.

We sat on the second floor huddled as near as possible to a small fire, our borrowed sweaters swathing our goose-pimpled shoulders, while we listened for an hour and a half to the reading of the day's book. My teeth were chattering like castanets; I feared they could be heard above the reading.

Our hostess said to me, kindly, that she hoped I wouldn't be chilly; she did not care for overheated houses. She did not care for taxis either, I heard later. When she and her very distinguished brother were invited out to dinner, *he* went by taxi while *she* went by streetcar. Yet she gave vast sums to her favorite charities.

This combination of extreme personal thrift and public benevolence is a not uncommon Boston trait. A strong Puritan heritage may account for it. It isn't that Bostonians don't enjoy a good tuck-in as well as the next one. Nobody can lay in food and drink with more relish than your good Bostonian, if somebody else is paying for it. But don't expect either gratitude or appreciation from the recipients. They reserve the right, while lapping up food and drink with the gusto of a professional pie-eater, to look down their noses at the host setting out such a spread.

"Lavish" is a dirty word in Boston.

Not long after my arrival I became entangled in a series of Sunday Afternoon Teas given by an elderly neighbor. I was never really sure why she asked me; we disagreed on every conceivable subject. But indulging her own perversities had become her great amusement. She enjoyed an argument. She would seat perhaps a dozen suitably conservative people around her large mahogany tea table and then throw out some remark like, "I feel we have been being *unreasonably rude* to the poor dear Russians." She would then sit back and bask in the fireworks.

To be asked to serve tea was a dubious honor; you starved. The antique silver teapot was a beautiful little piece, holding perhaps a pint of hot liquid at one time. You served three or four people, and then the maid, almost as antique as the pot, limped slowly downstairs to some subterranean hideout to fetch more. By the time she got back, the first-served had drunk their tea and were waiting impatiently in line with the ones who hadn't had any yet. You never got any refreshment yourself, and went home parched.

His method of dancing was to pick out a not too frequented spot on the floor, and then to revolve with increasing rapidity on that spot, like a top shot from a string.

Our hostess never noticed; she was supremely indifferent to any material comfort. Yet everything in the house was unique of its kind, like the exquisite little mahogany chairs people dragged up to the tea table.

I was unfortunately not present on the day a large and dignified grande dame sat on one and went through to the floor; but the scene was graphically described to me. The lady was hauled up by two gallant gentlemen who had considerable difficulty extricating her, since her far-from-scanty nether portions had become firmly embedded in the seat of her splintered chair.

But these teas paled beside the first Literary one I attended on Beacon Hill. In every literary gathering I had up to now attended, literature came first, tea later; it being a well-understood, if seldom mentioned fact that food and drink are always dispensed as a sort of reward for those who have stuck bravely by through the intellectual part of the afternoon.

Not here. Here, the order was courageously reversed. We were taken down one flight to a celestial basement dining room where a stupendous High Tea had been set out. There was hot chocolate in a great, wonderful china pot, with whipped cream; tea and coffee; paper-thin asparagus sandwiches, cookies, cakes, and plates of vanilla ice cream with huge ripe strawberries to be consumed as a sort of Crowning Touch to this magnificent supper — for supper it really was. This was such fare as poets seldom enjoy.

Skinny, ancient maids in immaculate uniforms darted about the room bearing trays of sandwiches and ice cream, urging more food on the not reluctant guests. I remember vividly one especially Mary Petty maid, her starched apron strings flying, scooching down with a plate of strawberries and ice cream under the hands of two gesticulating people and emerging triumphantly on the other side, her burden intact.

Fed, replete, and bursting at the seams with goodies, the entire party then ascended to the main floor. The inside wooden shutters, painted a dark gold, had been closed, leaving the old-fashioned double parlors in poetic cathedral gloom. Sitting carelessly on lacquer tables were large hunks of raw amethyst, figurines, superb little mother-of-pearl bibelots. From one wall protruded the head and neck of a large antique swan, possibly Florentine, of finely carved and painted white wood. On another hung a full-length Sargent portrait of our hostess.

It was she who opened the proceedings. In her eighties, still beautiful, standing before us she read, without the aid of eyeglasses, from some of her favorite ancient philosophers. She could have filled any theatre with her exquisitely modulated voice.

After this the poetry reading took place. Came the poetry; large doses of it, and not one person defected! No one took the opportunity to slip out! Truly, I began to see that Bostonians are cut from different stuff.

Once a year the little backyard gardens on Beacon Hill are opened, at a small price, for a Garden Tour which the public may attend. I was surprised to hear this event spoken of scornfully by the same lady who dispensed with heat in her house.

"Oh, not for me! All this rushing about at the last minute to stick a milk bottle with a daffodil in it in the ground!"

It was hardly a just comment; but there was, I found later, a reason for her bitterness towards garden showings. Years before, at a time when things were far more decorous than they are today, she had unwittingly caused a considerable scandal in Garden Club circles. Captivated by the gay informality of the little vine-covered café gardens of Italy, she decided to reproduce in her Beacon Hill garden some of this wayward European charm. She therefore caused long clotheslines to be strung out over her garden and, just before the Annual Tour of garden lovers arrived, she ordered hung up on the lines a casual array of her own immaculately laundered undergarments.

It was meant to be reproduction of a gay, informal Neapolitan scene; but somehow, in Boston, the effect was not quite the same. Moving about under a flapping cloud of Mrs. C's skivvies, Beacon Hill visitors felt distinctly ill at ease. Were you supposed to look? How could you *not* look?

It made history.

The Waltz Evenings are a great Boston institution, open to those socially eligible and terpsichoreally fit. We had the honor, shortly after our arrival in Boston, to be invited to one. Our host, a charming fellow in his early eighties (many of Boston's most delightful hosts are in their early eighties) was a skilled and inveterate waltzer. If my remembrance of the evening is not quite the glowing one I had anticipated, it is perhaps because of the very proficiency of our host.

His method of dancing was to pick out a small, not too frequented spot on the floor with the care of a male whooping crane selecting a favorable nesting site, and then, without ever leaving it, to revolve with

"I just walked back from the Symphony!" I shouted. "Yes, so did I," she said. "Bracing isn't it?"

increasing rapidity on this spot, like a top shot from a string. As we spun rapidly round and round, I could only try, whirling on my fractured toes, to keep my balance and stay on my feet. I had a terrifying vision of myself crashing to the floor in an unseemly tangle with my elderly cavalier, and I could imagine the uncharitable guesses made in this case by the other dancers on the amount of champagne I had presumably consumed to cause this catastrophe.

It seemed to me that my partner's gyrations, far from running down, increased in velocity as we went along. I felt that to others we must appear as a sort of imposing joint blur, like the blades of an airplane propeller. Was he carried along by the sheer force of his own momentum? Could he perhaps (the terrifying thought came to me suddenly) *not* stop?

Suddenly it was over. The music mercifully ceased. Perfectly calm, in full possession of his breath, our host said pleasantly, "Ah, there is Mrs. Galway. We must go over and speak to her."

I made my way beside him with a noticeable lurch in my gait. What she thought of me I shall never know; but I have the distinct impression that Mrs. Galway had two heads.

The Boston Symphony is one of the world's finest. But when I first came to Boston I was puzzled by the fact that on certain Fridays two or three people would call up to offer me their Symphony tickets; on other days, not a single one. It must, I thought, be accident; yet it was odd how often it happened.

It took me a little time, and not a few soakings, to discover that Bostonians read the weather reports with the attention with which others peruse astrological charts. On the day when a severe blizzard with four to six inches of heavy snowfall is predicted, a generous rain of Symphony tickets may be expected.

On one such afternoon, spent ensconced in somebody else's seat, I found on emerging that a really violent storm was raging; driving snow, howling winds, gusts of gale force. Even the MBTA was not running; a line of several hundred waiting people extended all the way out to the street. I wrapped my coat around me, shut my useless umbrella, and set out to walk home.

Stinging snow and hail blinded me, gale-force winds forced me to bend double, my rain hood was precious little protection. Reaching Beacon Hill at last, I struggled up it, proud of my rugged valor — and saw coming towards me an elderly lady in, at least, her late seventies, who

Though technically a question, it managed to cast aspersions on the speaker's integrity, knowledge, education and intentions. . . 

lives near me.

"I just walked back from the *Symphony*!" I shouted above the roar of the elements.

"Yes, so did I," she said casually. "Bracing, isn't it?"

I crept home, deflated.

One of the favorite indoor sports on Beacon Hill is attending Civic Association meetings to discuss neighborhood matters — a bridge, a turn-around, a new one-way street. These are definitely not to be missed. To see the adjoining citizenry streaking down to the Meeting House for one of these evening affairs, walking single-file like Indians on the warpath, brows bent, eyes glittering with purpose, is to realize Trouble is Brewing. The fact is, these neighborhood meetings are the modern equivalent of The Bear Pit. All is likely to go deceptively well for the Speaker until, lulled into a false sense of security by the truly flattering attention with which his words have been received, he winds up his address and asks if there are any questions.

Are there any questions! Long, long will he rue the asking of that one. Aside from an engraving of Custer's Last Stand, there is little to describe the ensuing scene. The inhabitants of Beacon Hill move in for the scalping en masse. Questions are shot at the Speaker from all sections of the floor, some from persons seated, some standing. Agitated hands, clamoring for attention, beat in the air like storm-tossed weather vanes.

The gentleman with the loudest voice usually gets the floor first. He has what is technically a question; but it manages to cast aspersions on the Speaker's integrity, knowledge, education and intentions.

The fact is, the residents of Beacon Hill, with a cunning born of long years of heckling at Civic Meetings, are experts at asking what purports to be a question while constituting a masterful rebuttal of everything the Speaker has said. Since questions have been invited, there is no way, short of lassoing the questioner and dragging him bodily off the floor, that the Speaker can silence him. Meanwhile the lady on his right is furiously signalling to be heard, and in back of her a red-faced gentleman is on his feet, trembling with rage, and on the other side of the aisle . . .

Afterwards, while the unfortunate Speaker is still wondering what hit him, refreshments are served in the basement. Virtuously thirsty from the public airing of their own ideas, Beacon Hillers lap up quarts of orange drink and coffee while chewing and spitting out bits of the Speaker. A thoroughly enjoyable time has been had by all, and nobody can wait for the next meeting.

No, Boston is never dull. It is not a place, like New York, where pleasure is a duty — but you would have to go a long way to find people more adept at turning duty into pleasure.

BEACON HILL: *Hub of the Universe*

BOSTON CLUBS

Pitfalls of the literary life. . .

BOSTON CLUBS

I suppose there are more different clubs in Boston than in any other city in the world. There must be a club for every taste, every occupation, unless you are a one-eyed kleptomaniac — (and for all I know, there may well be a club for one-eyed kleptomaniacs).

The problem, therefore, is not so much what club to join as what clubs to *avoid*. Everyone knows about the smart, expensive clubs, like the Somerset and Chilton — to belong to which one must have both impeccable social credentials and plenty of cash. But there are a host of other clubs — leaving out the Sewing Circles so dear to the hearts of a previous generation — some of which have been going on for over a hundred years. These embrace every kind of hobby and oddity, and are likely to demand not so much money as time.

A prize I had been fortunate enough to win shortly after my arrival in Boston was the cause of my being invited to attend a dinner at a certain club which had, if not currently famous members, at least a long-standing literary ancestry. I was invited about a month in advance, and was told that while I would be seated at the head table, I would not be required to speak.

It seemed as if a pleasantly carefree evening stretched ahead of me. It was with anticipation not unmixed with curiosity that I made my way into the hall on the appointed night.

The first thing that struck my eye were the ladies' wraps, as displayed in the cloakroom. Not since my great-grandmother's time has my eye fallen upon such superb vintage clothing. The average year appeared to be circa 1910. One or two of the ladies who were removing their outer wraps at the time I came in were wearing long dresses of purple velvet with high-boned lace collars.

I don't know why these costumes managed so poignantly to evoke what, in my grandmother's time, was meant by the word, "literary."

Tottering about a large hall, dominated by a long head table and a group of smaller round ones, were many congenial groups, largely female, with one or two white-haired, distinguished-looking gentlemen to every group. All, it would seem, were known to each other. As strangers, they regarded us with polite curiosity. One official-looking matron, bustling up, presented my husband and myself to the evening's master of ceremonies, a retired newspaperman with an immensely vague but charming manner.

"O yes yes yes," he murmured, "I remember now. So glad you could be with us. Your husband will be sitting at that round table there — with Mr. Mathews, the author of all those sea stories, you know. You will be sitting with us at the head table. Where are the others? . . . want you to meet some of them . . ."

I was introduced to several ladies who at one time or another had published articles (one on old china, one on gardening) in various newspapers, and to the very imposing Dean of a large university who had just had a book published. He was, I noted with relief, definitely going to speak. One could judge, after only a few moments' conversation with the Dean, that there would be little time left for any other speaker on a program which embraced the Dean's talents as an orator. Any lurking uneasiness that I might after all be asked to say a few words, vanished from my mind; I felt I could now definitely relax.

The babble of conversation rose. Little by little, a long gaggle of slightly nervous individuals had assembled at our table and were now standing behind it, making strained and desultory conversation.

"I think perhaps we should start dinner," our master of ceremonies, Mr. Franklin Lane, said vaguely. "Good deal past time now. Can't keep the waitresses, you know. Sit down, everybody, won't you?"

It was fortunate that nobody at our table obeyed this command literally, or we would all have landed heavily on the floor on our posteriors. No chairs whatsoever had been provided for the head table.

Once this oversight had been called to Mr. Lane's attention, a vast distressed scurrying took place. Various gentlemen from outlying tables brought their own chairs gallantly up; more were hastily dug out of the coat closet. Cautiously, we sat down. The dinner proceeded.

At about the ice-cream-and-chocolate-sauce stage, Mr. Lane rose to his feet and made a delightful, if slightly rambling, speech of welcome.

"Getting a bit senile, you know," the gentleman next to me somewhat superfluously confided. "Can't remember where he's at, good part of the time. But an *awfully* nice fellow."

Mr. Lane's method of choosing speakers fully bore out these remarks. There seemed to be no particular order to it — unless the catching of an eye between mouthfuls of ice cream was what triggered it. He skipped about from one end of the table to the other, calling on this or that one apparently at random.

Sticking studiously to my ice cream and chocolate sauce, I avoided

Mr. Lane's eye. When I heard him call out the Dean's name, I relaxed completely. Alphabetically, it was a long way below mine. I was assured of being Home Free.

The Dean made an excellent, if somewhat long-drawn-out speech, as Deans are likely to. It was received with hearty applause. I picked up my ice cream spoon again. In the middle of polishing off the last mouthful of chocolate sauce, I heard as through a bad dream Mr. Lane's voice saying, "And now, we will hear from our new visitor, who will tell us a little about her work. I'm sure we will all be interested to hear —" and my name called out.

That treacherous master of ceremonies had doubled back on his tracks and picked my "H" out of thin air, where he had previously been browsing among the "W's."

The victim of betrayal, no less than the Spartans at Thermopylae who looked up to see the glitter of enemy spears filtering through the yielded pass at their backs, I dropped my ice-cream spoon with a clatter on my saucer and struggled to my feet, to polite applause.

Clichés from thousands of less-than-memorable occasions thronged into my head and saved me.

"As guest of your distinguished Club," I began, "I am so happy to be with you tonight . . ."

It sounded, I noted with relief, like hundreds of other speeches.

It was.

BEACON HILL: *Hub of the Universe*

ON BOSTON CALLERS

Coming from New York was a social liability

When I first took up residence in Boston I spent two years waiting for someone to call. As soon as my glass curtains were up I became very nervous; would find myself, around four o'clock of a wintry afternoon, peering furtively out a corner of the window at likely-looking prospects coming up the street; and had the silver teapot polished to a perfection it has never attained before or since.

I even had crisp little biscuits laid out, which gradually mildewed over the days-to-come and attained a fine shade of penicillin green.

After a while I did indeed have callers. A random list included:

The representative of a local window-cleaning service.
A little boy selling chocolate cookies for the Boy Scouts.
Two girls looking for a street in Dorchester.
The Fuller Brush man, who left me a sample brush.
A representative of the United Fund, complete with stickers.
The little boy next door, who had lost his key.
A charming-looking couple who were hunting for friends down the street.
An elderly man with a pedigree reaching back to Charlemagne, which he recited while selling me two quarts of Black Walnut furniture polish.
Two policemen with tickets they were selling for the Policeman's Ball.

I think now that I was at least partly misled by the superlatively domestic-looking houses on the other side of the street. Brass-knockered, lace-curtained, iron-scrapered, their scraps of green lawn fenced in decorously with black iron railings, they looked the very picture of quiet family houses.

It took me some time to discover that, underneath their fine antique veneer, these domestic-looking dwellings were actually apartment-houses, containing as many layers of complete strangers as any comparable block in New York.

This is one of the deceptive things about Boston in general and Beacon Hill in particular. The old houses (which are, in fact, forbidden to change their exteriors under a recent Historical District zoning) so charming, so sedate, enter into a quiet conspiracy with their owners to keep the same outward appearance they have always had, even though complete strangers may be paying exorbitant rents for the second, third and fourth floors.

Rare indeed is the house now occupied exclusively by the same family.

There is a reason for this, a sound economic one. "Taxpayers" as these rented apartments are colloquially known, are a virtual necessity under Boston's ever-increasing tax burden. The desirability of living in as attractive a neighborhood district as Beacon Hill, combined with the limited area available, has shot the rents ever higher and resulted in people putting up with more inconveniences, for more money per capita, than perhaps any other place in the United States.

Where else would people pay an astronomical rent for the privilege of ascending four stories, pantingly, on foot, without benefit of elevator? Where else would young couples, wild to find any perch on Beacon Hill, be willing to exist precariously in basement apartments with pipes zigzagging crazily along the ceilings, kitchens which are merely electric plates concealed behind creaking doors, a multitude of trash cans from upstairs chummily cheek-by-jowl in the hallway? Not only live there, but pay a stiff rent to do so? (And if you can't do it alone, get in two other couples and a large police dog.)

No, The Hill definitely has something. But not necessarily privacy.

At a certain point in my first year I stopped worrying about the threat of callers; but I had been made a member of this and that, and well-disposed friends had been dragging me about.

Where else would people pay astronomical rent to live in basement apartments with pipes zigzagging crazily along the ceilings?

"She has only been in Boston a year," they would explain to our hostess. "She comes from New York."

This well-intended explanation, I slowly began to realize, was not the greatest assist to social popularity in Boston. It put me in what was apparently an untenable position at once.

I wish I could imitate the inevitable reply. It came in the form of a sort of soft, long-drawn-out whinny, delivered through the nose.

"Oh — *Real-ly?*" Indicating sympathy, disapproval, surprise mixed with a sort of patronizing commiseration.

New York. Really?

The next question was, inevitably, "And how do you like Boston?"

It gave one — nay, it demanded of one — the all-out opportunity to perjure one's soul.

More honest was a large friendly lady who, on being informed of my dispiriting situation, clasped my hand between both of hers and said, with sympathy, "Oh, you poor darling you!"

Bostonians, I have discovered, have a curious ambivalent feeling about New York. Officially they disapprove of it, they look down on it and are loud in their thankfulness that they don't have to live there; and they sneak away to visit it whenever they get the chance. They revel in the shops, the thousands of little restaurants, the plays; and enjoy the little put-down it enables them to give their more insular friends.

"Oh, yes, do go and see it! I'm sure you'll enjoy it. I saw it two months ago, in New York."

But — live in it? Heavens, no.

New York is a good place to visit.

BEACON HILL: *Hub of the Universe*

PARDON ME, BUT IS YOUR HOUSE ON FIRE?

I had enjoyed other people's fires, but never thought to provide one myself. . .

PARDON ME, BUT IS YOUR HOUSE ON FIRE?

Almost any good fire makes a pleasant social occasion on Beacon Hill — better than a cocktail party for renewing social acquaintance, with the added fillip of free entertainment thrown in. It is amazing how many people, unseen before, can stream in from all directions and clot the streets and sidewalks at the mere rumor of a fire.

I had myself enjoyed many other peoples' fires, but never thought to provide one. However, I did.

It was the middle of summer; our house therefore thought by the neighbors to be empty. However, we were going to Nantucket and had come back to pick up a few casual clothes. I was pressing a cotton skirt in the upstairs front bedroom with one of those fragile little travel irons — top-heavy with its cord but the only one I had available — when I went downstairs for something, leaving the iron on its safety-rest position on its rubber-and-asbestos ironing pad. While I was downstairs, the telephone rang.

It was a man with a long message for my husband. After I had written it down, the telephone rang again; this time it was a nephew.

In the middle of our conversation I began to be conscious of a disturbing sound. It was a sort of pulsing noise; glub, glug; glug, glug —

almost like water going through a pipe. Moreover, it seemed to be increasing in volume. I cut the conversation short.

"I'll have to hang up now, Jim; there's a sort of funny noise. Tom may have left a soldering iron on in his workshop."

I went downstairs to my husband's workshop and cast a suspicious look around. Nothing seemed to be wrong. I ran upstairs, suddenly acutely aware of the travel iron I had left on.

The wind had blown the door of the front bedroom shut. I threw it open.

It was a black world I looked into. The room was murky with thick dark smoke; it resembled something from Dante's Inferno. The whole ironing board, rubber cover and all, was in flames. What was left of the iron, still attached to its cord, was making the odd pulsating noise I had heard; the ironing board cover, advertised as fireproof, was not. Everything was a mass of licking fire. With the gutted iron in the center, it looked like one of those religious paintings in which you see a heart dramatically surrounded by flames.

My first impulse was to rush to the top of the stairs and bawl, like a

"You take that hose right out of there," I shouted from the window, the Housewife at Bay.

frightened heifer, for my husband, that arbiter *par excellence* of anything mechanical. (I have seen him start a refrigerator, out of order for two weeks, merely by kicking it.)

My next was the realization that, as always when some really dramatic crisis comes up, he was not in the house.

I have since been told that the worst and most dangerous thing I could have done was to disconnect the iron. This is what I did first. I wrapped my hands in several thicknesses of towel and pulled sharply. The plug came out with no trouble, and the pulsating sound ceased.

I then rushed to the bathroom and soaked several heavy bath towels which I brought back and hurled on the flames. As this did not quite extinguish them, I added a pink silk comforter from the bed. This combination dampened things enough to enable me to take up the whole smoldering mess and dump it into the bathtub, where I turned on the water.

But the heavy black smoke was everywhere. It seemed to have increased, if anything. So I turned on the big fan in the front window.

I did not know, busy as I was with the remnants of the ironing-board cover in the bathtub, that this caused a column of black smoke roughly the size of a 60-megaton atomic explosion at Los Alamos to mushroom out over the street, where it hung motionless in a heavy black cloud. I did not pause to reflect that the neighbors thought us still away and the house empty. I did not, in fact, dream that one of them had phoned the fire department in a panic and turned in an alarm.

But, over the sound of rushing water in the bathtub, I fancied I heard a ring at the doorbell and going down, found a stout lady standing on my front steps.

"Pardon me," she said politely, "but is your house on fire?"

"No, it's not," I said, and added, mindful of my manners, "but thank you for asking."

"I'm sorry to have troubled you," she apologized, turning away. "But all that black smoke . . ."

Before closing the door, I uttered a statement that must have completed the good lady's bemusement.

"It's the *rubber* , you see," I said, and shut the door.

Busy as I was swabbing out the bathtub, I must have missed the arrival of the fire engines by a good ten minutes.

A shattering crash of timbers below street level awakened me to the fact that all was not well. I rushed to the window and looked out.

What appeared to be the entire Boston fire department, helmeted and rubber-booted, was following ten miles of heavy hose straight through our shattered basement doorway. I shouted from the window, the Housewife at Bay.

"You take that hose right out of there! Stop it at once!"

It was only then I became conscious of the size of the crowd now gathered in front of our abode. It seemed to stretch in all directions, like one of those odd nightmares in which everyone you have ever known is, somehow, all at once present.

Prominently in the forefront was the neighbor who had turned in the alarm, a baby slung on each hip like a six-shooter. My neighbors on the other side, a couple we know down the street, and [illegible] brother-in-law from out of town (how had he gotten here?), a sister-in-law from neighboring Chestnut Street, as well as a horde of assorted friends, neighbors, and strangers, were all gathered below, peering up at me like so many fish, their mouths agape.

Nobody said a word. Nobody volunteered so much as a glass of water to pour on the flames; they all stood staring with the rapt and avid expectancy of people prepared and ready at any moment to see a succession of lifeless corpses carried out in blankets.

Meanwhile, smoked out, if I may use the phrase, by my bellows, a sort of Little Caesar of the Fire Department had emerged from the basement, obviously in charge.

"You take all that stuff out of here!" I shouted. "The very idea of smashing in our door!"

"Madam" he said coldly, "we were sent for. To put out a fire."

"Well, there *isn't* any fire. It was only my traveling iron."

"Take me to it!" he commanded with the air of an emperor.

We tramped upstairs together, a file of eight or ten stout rubber boots and myself. Without a word, we looked at the black and smoking towels. Silently we inspected the wrecked remains of the ironing board — including, I was pained to note, a large black charred place on the floor.

Little Caesar then picked up a small, still-smoldering rug and heaved it bodily out the window. It was his revenge and his swan song; they all left.

I went downstairs and found my husband with his mouth full of nails, a large hammer in his hand, banging away at the shattered frame of our cellar door.

"I had a fire!" I shouted accusingly, "and you weren't here!"

"Sure, I know," he said casually. "Heard about it two blocks away."

It seemed to me that it would have been more fitting for him to be clasping me to his bosom, sobbing out his relief that he hadn't found his adored one a cinder, instead of whanging the door back into place with a heavy sledgehammer.

But that's Boston for you. After all, I got him here.

BEACON HILL: *Hub of the Universe*

THE BOSTON ATHENAEUM

Apparitions among the Gilbert Stuarts and the Copleys

One of the oldest private libraries in the country, the Athenaeum is a splendidly Boston institution.

There are no signs, as in public libraries, saying, "SILENCE!" There don't have to be. The Athenaeum habitués understand well the unwritten rules. The only sound, in the sunny first-floor reading room where magazines from all over the world are neatly laid out on counters, is the occasional rustle of a turning page by one of the absorbed gentlemen who daily come to do their reading there.

I do not know what would happen to anybody so ill-advised as to start a loud conversation in this inner sanctum. It is my impression that various elderly gentlemen would simply glide out from their solitary nooks and throw him out the nearest window, then return wordless to their interrupted reading.

Of massive brownstone, with magnificent heavy bronze doors, the Athenaeum even *looks* like an Institution of Learning. Set back in dignified fashion from Beacon Street, a small flight of steps leads up to its marble-floored interior. Here at a desk sit several charming and omniscient librarians who write down the numbers of your books, telephone up for others, and receive returns from a discreet dumbwaiter arrangement in back.

The Athenaeum, which started out in life as a combined library and art gallery, possesses some remarkably fine paintings — Gilbert Stuarts, Washington Allstons, Copleys et al. — along with such sculpture as Antoine Houdon's bust of George Washington and numerous marble busts of well-known Boston characters — among them the lovely head and shoulders of Emily Marshall, famous Boston beauty with whom half the city was in love. It also is rich in those tufts of culture dear to the Victorian heart — large oil paintings of the kind stored in the basement of most museums, etchings and drawings of various literary lights who once honored Boston with their presence, pedestaled carvings of prominent Boston businessmen — mute testament to the extraordinary democracy of marble.

An elevator stashed away at the back of the first floor takes you up to the Art Reference Room on the second floor, where are some of the handsomest paintings, as well as a magnificent chess set laid out on a table in the form of protagonists in "Alice in Wonderland," with a Bishop suspiciously resembling the late Cardinal O'Connell.

The third floor goes in for new acquisitions and cataloguing; the fourth floor reference department is beautifully housed, with long tables and alcoves for reading.

But it is the fifth floor which has what must be the most delightful reading-room in the country — running the full length of the building, flooded with sun from its many great glass windows, and commanding a superb view of the Old Granary Burial Ground. This room has, opening out from its high glass doors, a balcony where readers may sit in summer, absorbing sun and air along with their favorite books. It also has, opening on either side of its long center aisle, smaller recesses with tables where one can comfortably sit and read, or scribble if one has a mind to. It is a pleasant, civilized, scholarly place, with something meditative and monastic about it.

But the Athenaeum, like everything else, is changing. Gone are the days when, for the moderate sum of 15 cents, one could of an afternoon obtain a cup of tea and two crackers. ("Or four, if anyone wants to make a pig of himself," the former Director remarked tartly, in a private news-

He was slight, elderly, with thin spectacles slipping precariously off the end of his long nose; clad in a shabby old dressing gown and worn bedroom slippers.

sheet detailing the Athenaeum's privileges.)

However, this particular custom, if not quite at the same price, may be due for a revival; and there is at the moment a pleasant practice of an opening-day reception, with sherry, crackers and cheese, for some featured artist or writer.

But the little upper room at the head of a small flight of iron stairs, where one could sequester oneself in complete privacy and enjoy the privilege of typing on one's own typewriter, is divested forever of the presence of an elderly character who, I am told by a reliable witness, used to keep an old dressing gown and bedslippers hanging up there for his own particular comfort.

The lady who told me this recounted that she, sitting at a table reading one day, glanced up and saw, blinking in the light from the balcony, an apparition who resembled nothing so much as an Arthur Rackham drawing of Mr. Mole, from *The Wind in the Willows.* He was slight, elderly, with thin spectacles slipping precariously off the end of his long nose; and was clad in a shabby old dressing gown and worn bedroom slippers.

He stood, gazing down uncertainly at the scene below, until he happened to catch my friend's unbelieving stare; when like a disturbed small animal he slipped quickly back into his burrow and disappeared, leaving her wondering if she had imagined this apparition.

Inquiry on her part revealed that what she had witnessed was, for Athenaeum employees, a quite usual sight, to which they had grown completely accustomed.

Those of us who have not the distinction of being one of the Proprietors of the Athenaeum, and attending their monthly meetings, must be content with a guest card provided by some generous friend, which entitles us to book-borrowing privileges and the use of the Reading Room — no mean gift in itself.

But ah to be a Proprietor, turn up at the Monthly Meetings and give voice to one's opinions there!

My elderly neighbor of the assorted tea parties across the street had been for many years a Proprietor of the Athenaeum and enjoyed, I must believe, a slightly sadistic pleasure from turning up regularly at the meetings and tossing mental bombshells into their midst. She questioned everything and everybody, accepted nothing, and delighted in offering suggestions so bizarre that she could not have imagined they would ever be accepted, and must have offered them with the sole mischievous motive of upsetting the apple cart and throwing everything into confusion.

It is a tribute to the stamina and long-suffering Christian rectitude of the other Proprietors that invitations to attend were never withheld from her.

BEACON HILL: *Hub of the Universe*

BELLES LETTRES IN BOSTON

Where poets and nature meet head on

One of Robert Frost's best-known poems begins, "Something there is that doesn't love a wall."

If I may paraphrase this famous line, it is equally true that, "Something there is that doesn't love a poet."

I'm afraid it's practically everything.

Just let a poetry reading be announced for a certain date — just let the notice be printed in the newspapers and a number of people signify their intention of going, and watch what the weather will cook up on that day. If there hasn't been any snow up to then, this announcement will certainly bring the first blizzard of the winter howling in. If summer, rain in absolute cloudbursts can be expected, usually accompanied by thunder and lightning as the speaker mounts the podium.

In fact poets, who do nothing but praise nature in verse, seem in some way to have deeply outraged it.

New England, of course, has more opportunity for this type of Boreal Spite than most other parts of the country. But I am convinced that Arizona could produce a good dust storm, Mississippi a first-rate flood, Alaska the worst kind of williwaw, were a poetry reading to be an-

Poets, though they praise nature in verse, seem in some way to have deeply outraged it. . .

nounced in any of these regions. Somewhere up in the sky is a rejected poet — you can't tell me — with a spite against the whole genre.

If it isn't the weather, then it's one of man's own inventions. A fire engine, a factory whistle, a loud repetitive police siren, will suddenly surface from nowhere to silence a poet. I have known a steamer to let go with a five-minute blast just as the evening's bard started to speak, when nobody even suspected, up to then, that there were any boats in the vicinity.

Church bells are good silencers; so are striking clocks with brassy gongs. A loud TV set, even a telephone ringing persistently and unanswered, will compete successfully for the audience's attention.

This is perhaps an age when the human voice isn't meant to be heard.

And yet poets, with their extraordinarily ill-conceived desire to project their own, will continue to fight it.

Sometimes, in the case of a poet of great distinction and a commanding number of years, the weather will relent a little. Then the fretful burden of man-made sound will take up the challenge.

On the memorable occasion when the Boston Arts Festival invited Marianne Moore, considered by many to be America's leading female poet, to speak in the Public Garden, there was present a crowd of something like five thousand persons, sprawled rank after rank on little wooden chairs in the semidarkness under the elms. We watched the flocks of errant seagulls meander leisurely in over the streaked silver sky, observed the lights on the bridge slowly turn from pearl to diamond, and waited for Miss Moore.

At last the brisk, energetic young man who always announces celebrities in the vocal capital letters common to radio and TV announcers appeared on the little platform, shot the microphone up and down like a jack-in-the-box, and in hushed accents let us know that Miss Moore was now in our immediate suburbs, as it were, and would presently be with us.

The vast waiting crowd, containing in its depths almost every element of the reading public — long-haired collegiates, girls with shirttails hanging out over their shorts, pipe-smoking professors and avid, bearded young Activists of one sort or another — heaved an anticipatory sigh and settled back to wait.

It cannot be claimed that Miss Moore, faced with the challenge of this bumper audience, made a grand and stately entrance in the manner of Queen Elizabeth the Second or even Zsa Zsa Gabor. She walked briskly on, rather like a beloved aunt, expected for lunch, who has brought with her the promised spongecake to go with the strawberries.

And like the favorite aunt, she appeared to be encumbered with various burdens of which she wished at once to disembarrass herself. The fact that something like 5000 interested spectators were watching her do it had, you felt, not the remotest interest for her.

Someone handed her, as she came on stage, one of those huge and terrifying bunches of stiff, long-stemmed red roses always given out, usually by a petrified small girl in a starched white dress, at ship launchings and the arrival of foreign royalty.

Miss Moore accepted these graciously and got rid of them at once. As a matter of fact, she handed them to the young man who had introduced her — not with any awkward haste, but simply with the casual speed of someone getting rid of a wet mackerel — no hard feelings, but *you* hold it.

She appeared to be garbed in a sort of black velvet cloak — it may not have been velvet, but you felt it was, or *should* be velvet — which she shrugged off, and deposited in the deferential arms of still another young man, who took it with the air of one accepting, with awe, the last offspring of a royal line.

I believe she had on, under this, a heavy suit jacket which she also removed, depositing it in the arms of still another young man. (At one time the stage seemed to be full of deferential young men, surrounding Miss Moore as its packers do some precious objet d'art — or perhaps as did Queen Elizabeth the First's clique of elegant young courtiers.)

Miss Moore dismissed them not so much with any outward or overt gesture as by a sort of tacit spiritual settling-down and smoothing of ruffled feathers by which she let us know that she was at last with us, unencumbered with burdens and able to be completely herself. When she spoke, it was in the unhurried voice of one continuing an interrupted conversation with a next-door neighbor.

It would be impertinent for one not having made careful notes to try to quote Miss Moore verbatim, and besides it would be impossible; her style is her own and probably not duplicable.

As nearly as I can remember, her remarks went something like this, delivered in the unraised voice of someone making a casual aside to a favorite nephew: "Well. I've been asked to read a poem for the Boston Arts Festival, so I thought I would begin with what I wrote just *for* the Festival. This is it."

At once, summoned as always from the Nether Regions by the very mention of Belles Lettres, three or four bright red fire engines appeared from nowhere and began racing wildly about the outer confines of the Public Garden, sirens at full flood; a succession of planes in sharp ascent, engines roaring, passed overhead; a child began to howl and a dog to bark.

Nobody in the crowd at the Public Garden heard them at all. Bent forward in our seats, eyes fixed on the modest little figure on the stage, Miss Moore held us, insulated from all extraneous sensation, in the hollow of her hand.

BEACON HILL: *Hub of the Universe*

WHY DO WE ALWAYS STOP AND SMILE AT EACH OTHER WHEN WE MEET?

The tricky etiquette of street-greetings. . .

WHY DO WE ALWAYS STOP AND SMILE AT EACH OTHER WHEN WE MEET?

I have an elderly neighbor to whom I have been introduced more than once, with the proper explanation, or apology: "She lives right below you, Miss B!"

"She does WHAT?"

"SHE LIVES RIGHT BELOW YOU! JUST A FEW HOUSES DOWN!"

"Oh, indeed."

She doesn't seem tremendously bucked up to find I am living right below her; indeed, though she doesn't go so far as to say so out loud, I have the uneasy feeling she thinks the whole neighborhood is going down, and this is just another proof of it.

Meeting her on the street, she looks at me rather woodenly, even a little suspiciously, as I smile and bow; it is quite obvious that she does not remember ever seeing me before and wonders why an absolute stranger is bestowing on her this silly greeting. One day, indeed, driven by an unexpected surge of curiosity, she stopped dead in front of me and demanded, "Why do we always stop and smile at each other when we meet on the street?"

I was glad to know she considered she was smiling; I had not guessed as much; and I was tempted to reply with some frivolous answer, like, "Because we're both so irresistibly beautiful."

But I know better. A few wintry Boston encounters have nipped the more giddy buds of speech in me. I remain on the sensible plain of fact.

Once, however, we found a common meeting ground, she and I; and it was, of all things, a poodle.

I had before observed that she had a certain weakness for dogs, while walking a neighbor's poodle about the Hill; she had stopped to greet affectionately, not me, but the poodle.

On this occasion, at dusk on a wintry day when a light snow had fallen and lain just long enough on the ground to become soiled, melting and slushy, I saw, lying ahead of me on a path in the Public Garden, a white poodle. Or what had been a white poodle. Its collar was worn and dirty and covered with snow, the fur on its belly wet and draggled as from long wandering, and it lay, blocking the path, as if either dead, dying or too exhausted to care what happened to it.

It is unusual to find a poodle without an owner attached. A hound, a police dog, any kind of mongrel one may find wandering loose and ownerless; but not a poodle.

Particularly a white poodle. Either because they are expensive dogs, or because they are intelligent and charming house pets who automatically become members of the family, poodles are seldom alone. This one, in its exhaustion, its bedraggled state and the demoralized way in which it had let itself sprawl out on a mat of dirty melting snow, had all the sad earmarks of that most forlorn of all living creatures, a Lost Dog.

I stopped dead in front of it and looked down at the bedraggled animal. I then became aware that somebody else, approaching from the other side, had done exactly the same thing. I looked over at her through the gathering dusk and perceived that it was my neighbor, Miss B.

It is not in her nature to beat about the bush.

"Your dog?" She shot the inquiry at me like a hockey puck.

Two can play at that game. "Never saw it before," I snapped.

"It looks lost."

"Just what I thought."

I bent, and fumbled at the collar of the not-very-cooperative animal. "Let's see if it has a license."

Some day I shall be severely bitten while fumbling, as I constantly am, at the collar of a strange dog; but that divine Providence which is said to look after lunatics has so far been kind. I found the license, and with difficulty spelled it out in the gathering dark. "It says C-45380. And wait, there's a name and address here — Jane Buskin, 45 Charles."

"That's not far from here," my neighbor said. "In fact, it must be right next door to where my plumber lives. We must call the owner at once — she must be frantic about the animal. Have you a pencil to write down the name? I am on my way home now, and can call her up the moment I get there."

Fumbling in my bag, I located a ball-point pen but nothing to write on except a check, which I sacrificed to Kindness to Animals; tearing the check in two and handing the name and license number to Miss B. I then continued on my way to do a last-minute errand at Shreve's. Coming back with my box of writing paper clutched in my hand, I looked for the dog, and was no little relieved to find him gone, as I had had visions of having to carry him, wet and draggled as he was, up The Hill. One could hope that Miss B had zeroed in on her humanitarian task. I went home and set about preparing dinner.

Buoyed up by all this cordiality, it was with a self-confident smile that I greeted Miss B the next time we met on the street.

The telephone rang, and the sound of Miss B's stentorian voice filled the kitchen. "Hello. Hello. Mrs. H? This is your *neighbor,* Jane B. I wanted to tell you that the poodle is safe. Its owner, the young woman who lives on Charles Street" (Miss B did not have to tell me what she thought of any young woman deliberately selecting Charles Street as a residence) "tells me that the dog is a great wanderer; it has been known to go as far on one of its excursions as Kenmore Square. She has great difficulty keeping it at home. She went out at once and secured it after I called her. I telephoned her again to make sure she had. And you know something amusing? That scrap of paper you found in your bag to write on was a *check!* The part you gave me had your name and address on it! That's how I was able to call you. You are a *neighbor* of mine. Isn't that a coincidence? You live right below me."

"I do?"

"Yes. We even use the same bank. I consider all this a *most* amusing coincidence!"

Buoyed up by all this cordiality, it was with a self-confident smile that I greeted Miss B the next time we met on the street. I felt that we had at last breached the sound barrier and become friends.

But she looked at me woodenly, without expression, without speaking. Then, apparently driven by an unexpected surge of curiosity, she turned and said, "Tell me — why do we always stop and smile at each other when we meet on the street?"

BEACON HILL: *Hub of the Universe*

YELLOW DIAMONDS ON A BUS

Some hide their light under a bushel, some under cotton gloves. . .

YELLOW DIAMONDS ON A BUS

If you ask a Boston lady, particularly an unmarried Boston lady, to do something on the spur of the moment, you are almost certain to be turned down. They don't *do* things on the spur of the moment — their days are likely to be planned weeks in advance, and (it is my impression) they are a little miffed at your assumption that they might be free at the last moment to accept any engagement whatsoever. The Reading Club Monday, the Hospital Committee Tuesday, the Morning Lectures Wednesday — so it goes. Not a moment is foolishly left to chance.

Moreover, they prefer to make all cultural expeditions in pairs, whether it's Symphony Friday afternoon or a bus-chartered expedition to Winterthur — they go with an old friend (indeed, they have no others) and are thus assured not only of congenial company but, almost as important, are protected automatically from the danger of being thrown with *un*congenial company.

Aware as I had become of this tribal custom, I still, during my first year in Boston, decided on the spur of the moment to join a chartered bus load of ladies from the Women's Educational and Industrial Union who were riding to Worcester to see a New England Arts and Crafts Show featuring fine jewelry-work. As I was taking a course in metalwork myself, my wrists jingling with homemade silver bracelets, I decided it was worth braving the disapproval of an unknown bus load of strange ladies to see the show. With a brave face, therefore, ticket clutched in hand, I mounted the steps of the bus, which seemed to be packed to the very back with austere, high-minded-looking ladies sitting decorously two by two, like the animals in the Ark — all of whom stared at me suspiciously, or so it seemed to my self-conscious fancy — as I bolted to the rear of the bus alone.

Fortune favors the brave. Sitting alone near the back of the bus was a gentle-looking little lady in a worn cotton dress and well-washed white cotton gloves. To my timid, "Are you saving this seat for someone?" she gave a gracious negative, and moved aside her straw handbag so that I could sit down. I even fancied she seemed a little relieved herself — we now each had a seatmate. The whole bus was divided into seemly pairs. With a heave and a rattle it started, lurching up Boylston Street in the general direction of Worcester.

The bus now hummed with high-pitched female talk. My seatmate and I entered into a cautious, highly-generalized conversation. My first trip of this kind? Hers also. She had decided at almost the last moment to go. (This explained the lack of a female companion.) Her two sisters were due tomorrow from Jamestown, Rhode Island.

Rhode Island is where I spend my summers; this led by degrees to a discovery of mutual acquaintances. My seatmate relaxed noticeably and the conversation became more personal. Was I interested in jewelry? I was indeed. I explained my metalwork and displayed a bracelet. My companion warmed to my dubious expertise and put a hand on one shabby white cotton glove.

"Then," she said, "you may be interested in seeing this."

She stripped off the glove. A great flash of golden glitter struck me in the eye and temporarily blinded me. The stone on her finger extended from the base to well past the first knuckle. I have never seen such a many-faceted beam of light, so much concentrated sun. I sat staring at it while she complacently extended her finger, rigid, for my admiration. I started to say, "What a magnificent topaz!"

But something — some saving instinct, perhaps the regal pose of her little finger before me, which seemed to call for something more than the ordinary compliment — froze the words on my lips. In a small, uncertain voice, I said, "Is it . . . is it a yellow diamond?"

She nodded complacently. "It is indeed," she said. "A quite unique jewel, I believe — Tiffany's, in New York, would give anything to have it. An aunt of mine had a quite famous collection of jewels. She told me, before she died, that she was leaving this yellow diamond to me. 'Of course,' she said, 'you will sell it.' "

"But I have no intention of selling it. I get a great deal of pleasure out of wearing it, and wear it I shall."

I stared at my small, frail, elderly companion with growing wonder and admiration. People have been brutally murdered in cold blood for jewels infinitely less valuable than the one she was wearing under those rubbed cotton gloves.

"A friend to whom I showed this said to me, 'what a handsome topaz!' " my seatmate said, in accents of distinct though gentle disdain. "I said to her, 'You may *think* it a topaz, if you wish.' "

(I hugged myself at my narrow escape. It was obvious that my seatmate had expected me to recognize at once the quality of the stone.)

And yet she was wearing on her frail person a gem that any half-experienced thief would have known at a glance represented a lifetime's booty to whoever laid hands on it. Was she safe?

I looked at her thoughtfully. Who would dream that under those shabby, well-rubbed cotton gloves a fortune was hidden?

If one chooses to wear a priceless yellow diamond on one's finger through the streets, one could perhaps nowhere in the world find a better disguise than the one my little friend was wearing. If anyone on that bus was safe, she was. I mentally saluted both the yellow diamond and its owner.

BEACON HILL: *Hub of the Universe*

HOW TO REMOVE RUBBER DAISIES FROM THE BOTTOM OF YOUR BATHTUB

A playground for the female psyche

Among the many learned and erudite columns which grace the Boston newspapers, there is one which is unique; a playground for the Female Psyche to run Berserk in; a guide, not only to any physical problems which may arise around the home, but to the assorted problems of the heart as well. Unknown to each other by true name (for in these columns, pseudonyms are the rule) a whole generous and disinterested sisterhood is ready to rise in a body with wise and healing counsel for any female in distress.

There is literally no problem that this massed sisterhood has not at one time or another encountered.

Have you a bed-wetting child? An erring husband? A little boy who enjoys thwacking his head against the wall? A dog with the mange? A plant with spots? A live-in mother-in-law? A sloppy daughter? A disobedient son?

Are your neighbors rude, or over-friendly? Is a barking dog left out in the yard next door all night?

A friendly sisterhood, eager to give advice, has the answer to all these questions and many more: where to find a good clock-repairer, who still keeps metal Soap-Savers, what store specializes in Size E shoes, how to conceal a nasty scratch on the dining room table. I have personally tried many of their practical prescriptions, and can testify that the ladies are infallible.

Over our second cup of coffee of a morning, what store of riches spreads out before us! The names signed to the letters alone give some idea of the range of feminine imagination here displayed.

"Humpty Dumpty," "Worn Thin," "Star Fire," "Idyll in Freeport," "Cast Iron," "Blue Flamingo," "Watertown Louise," "Dotalou," "Sad Mother," "Skoal Troll," "Pink Chiffon," "Happy Squares," "Two Turtle Ladies," "Birdie of Lexington," "May Child," "Chicken Cherry," "Gazing Backward," "Owl Eyes," "Gerry Tonks," "Bag a Duffs," "Painted Home," "Pink Petunias," "Bedford English Rose," "Had a Ball," "Walpole Spirit of '76."

I had always assumed that the characters who select names for racehorses had a monopoly on far-out fancy until I encountered the magnificent collection in the Women's Pages. I can report triumphantly that we ladies have the racehorses skun a mile.

The writers possess, too, an undeniably lively style, and a refreshing lack of pedantic inhibitions about skipping blithely from one subject to another as fancy dictates.

Here is, "Another Me Too," answering an appeal from, "Sad Mother":

"I went through the same crisis with my husband ten years ago. I forgave him, with the aid of prayer and God's help. Has anyone a good recipe for Chocolate Chip Cookies?"

That, I think, puts the Erring Husband problem nicely in its proper place.

Or take the wide range of interest displayed by "Beauty of Blue" in commenting on a favorite preacher:

"Would there be any other readers who have been inspired by the spirituality of this great Man of God? Does anyone know where I can buy Texcraft Underwear in the City of Boston?"

"Dotalou," with personal problems of her own, is nevertheless generous:

"I enclose a recipe for the best pecan pie I ever ate. Can anyone recommend a good wax for the removal of hairs from the upper lip?"

"Watertown Louise" has creative ideas to offer:

"Why don't carpenters make bird houses to match peoples' houses?

To "Concerned Mamma": "I've heard that a child who is a head-banger is often musically inclined."

A laudable willingness to experiment in the cause of Better Living is a conspicuous feature of this column, as exemplified by a lady writing in on a canine problem.

"I don't know if Brewer's Yeast works on human hair, but it cures mange on dogs. I'd like to add my vote for soaking eggshells in water to use as plant food. My African Violets never looked better."

Understandably — considering the wide range of her activities — this lady signs herself, "Dog Tired."

With the daily accounts of worldwide disaster hurtling at us from all directions, and the prophets of doom threatening us hourly with calamities we are powerless to do anything about, what a relief to turn to our Chatters columns and find ourselves in a familiar world with which our particular female talents can cope!

No wonder, leaving the gloomy headlines and the crowded sports pages to our husbands, we flip the pages blithely over and are off to our own private Never-Never land. No detail too small, no subject too large but that we females, at home on our own territory, can have a go at it.

Here are discussed everything from Wayward Husbands (they must be forgiven; after all, we know the frailty of men and the temptations they are exposed to) to how to remove rubber daisies from the bottom of the bathtub. (You use a strong cleaning fluid and open the windows as wide as possible.)

After skimming over this column, the day looks less complicated. Others have coped triumphantly with the same problems; so can we. And meantime, it's not a bad time to polish off that second cup of coffee.

BEACON HILL: *Hub of the Universe*

FILENE'S BARGAIN BASEMENT

Down where the markdowns are knockdowns

Filene's Bargain Basement is world-famous. Noel Coward wrote a poem to it (which Filene's proudly printed in its next ad). Travelers from abroad make seeing it one of their first requests. I myself once helped a visiting Admiral's wife select dozens of rainbow-hued nylon negligées to take back with her as gifts to friends on Taiwan.

Filene's, of course, never prints its address. Among the difficulties a newcomer to Boston must cope with is the assumption of the advertisers that certain facts must be known to everybody, therefore need not take up space in print — such as the location of the principal stores. It is maddening to a newcomer to see a department store taking a whole page of a city newspaper to advertise what looks like a particularly enticing sale, without ever mentioning the address of the store which is having it.

This is because you are supposed to *know* the address of Bonwit's, Filene's, Jordan's, S.S. Pierce et al. as you know the location of the Pole Star. Hence, no space is wasted in printing up the obvious. When Filene's Bargain Basement is having a sale, it is assumed The Faithful will turn out.

What is more, they do. Promptly at 9:30 of a Monday morning, the carnage starts. In the advertising columns of the Sunday papers, The Faithful have read the good news. They have gone to bed early to be in good shape for combat, and streamed in, by bus, car and MBTA, to be the first in line, standing with their noses pressed against the glass doors at the very foot of the stairs emptying into the lower basement.

To look up from this desirable post is to panic. Jammed on the stairs as high as the eye can reach, like one of those early religious paintings showing the virtuous ascending into heaven, are rows of tight-packed females, lips compressed, bags clamped against bosoms, all set to leap forward on the first stroke of the bell that signals 9:30. The fervor in their eyes, while definitely there, is far from religious. If one should fall, one might be trampled to death.

But the mob is too tight-packed to fall. At the sound of the 9:30 bell and the opening of the glass doors by two apprehensive sales clerks who jump aside hastily, the crowd pours through the opened doors in one surging mass, scuttles down the aisles, hurtles around the main staircase in the middle and falls on the racks of marked-down dresses like a swarm of locusts on a green field, leaving them stripped and bare in a matter of moments.

However, to the cognoscenti, all is not lost even if the racks have temporarily been stripped bare. They may come back a day and a half later, when the Returns are in, the racks again full.

Not in the orderly fashion of the first day, it is true. There will be a wool suit here, a chiffon afternoon dress there, a satin evening jacket with a smooch on the sleeve next to a pants suit in striped beige. Here a fourteen, there a twelve, with an eight sandwiched in between. There is a species of ghoul which snips the expensive buttons from costly outfits; some of the more fragile fabrics will bear the mark of footprints where they have been dropped on a dusty floor.

No matter! Here is where the gemstones are to be found. If you know your clothes, rare, indeed, is the hunting here.

Once you become addicted to Filene's Bargain Basement, you are hooked — like Persephone's visit to the Underworld, it's a permanent thing — you can never really shop above-ground for long again.

I know women who have closets full of Filene's clothes they have never worn. It becomes an addiction, like taking drugs.

Filene's clothes? What am I talking about? They are clothes *bought* at

I have seen customers, veterans of an all-morning sale, wandering about in punch-drunk fashion, forgetting what they had come in for.

Trying on a dress, you stand upon your umbrella; you never put down your purse...

Filene's Bargain Basement, but they hail from distinguished stores all over the world. How else would I be able to sport about in hand-woven Irish tweeds, English linens and Scottish cashmere sweaters, to say nothing of famous designers' gowns from Paris, New York and Rome? (All previous labels are supposed to be cut out of the garments, but one finds labels along the inner seams or crossed out upon previous price tags — enabling one to plunk down forty dollars, say, and walk out with that three-hundred-dollar look.)

If Filene's Bargain Basement ever goes out of business, so will I. I will not be able to show my size 12 in public without the borrowed elegance of my marked-down clothes.

The most surprising people are Regulars at these sales. I have seen one of the most fashionable young matrons in Boston burrowing skillfully through a rack, tossing a great spray of chiffon evening gowns over her left shoulder as she did so. And there is one Grande Dame from Cambridge who regularly meets the chill winds in a long black velvet gown and wide black velvet hat. It is her uniform. Then why does she haunt Filene's B.B. of a Monday? Do such styles turn up now and then, cast up on her beach every so often by the tides of fashion? Impossible to know anything but that one can regularly meet her there of a Monday morning.

Occasionally Filene's breaks its own records. It made the newspaper columns with a sale of Russian Crown Sable coats at $10,000 each.

"Only one to a customer!" the advertisement announced, with commendable insouciance. "Original Price: $20,000."

A pretty young matron of my acquaintance spent part of the day before tripping in and out of the various entrances (of which Filene's has more than any rabbit warren) timing the speed required for each separate approach. She finally settled on one that led directly down, from two long flights of stairs, to the bowels of the Lower Basement, from which she only needed a short, straight dash to the arena of combat.

She was, she said, poised at the entrance at exactly five minutes of nine, making her first in line when the doors were flung open at 9:30.

I was vastly impressed by her scientific approach.

"And what did you buy?"

"Oh, I didn't *buy* anything! It was just fun to try on all those lovely sables."

Now that Filene's has been compelled to give up having dressing rooms (because, alas, too many light-fingered ladies abused the privilege) it is more difficult to select, without taking it home, a well-fitting gown. This does not deter certain customers who can be seen in front of the crowded mirrors struggling to pull a low-cut satin evening gown over a heavy wool suit. ("Would you mind zipping me up in back, dearie? I just *have* to know if this fits.")

If anyone took the trouble to film some of the scenes daily taking place in Filene's B.B., he would put all legitimate comedy instantly out of business.

One thing that must quickly be realized is that the famous sales attract probably the lightest fingers in town. Trying on a dress, you stand upon your umbrella; you never put down your purse. I once turned towards the cash register with a new purchase, leaving for a second a paper bag containing an already-paid-for satin slip. By the time I whirled back, remembering, the bag was gone.

Verbal, furious battles take place at each large Filene's sale.

"Excuse me. I'm ver-ree sor-ree, I'm sure," comes from a well-dressed woman who has just knocked an evening gown to the floor from the arm of the woman carrying it.

"It's all right to say you're *sorry,*" the wronged one snaps, out of breath from bending to pick it up. "If you're so sorry, whyn't you pick it up?"

"I *said* I was sorry. Why d'you keep on yapping about it?"

What probably saves actual physical combat from taking place is the crowds constantly pushing in between the two combatants. This is the only constant in Filene's B.B. After a morning spent at a really rewarding sale you stagger out so pummeled by elbows, so tired from carrying a batch of heavy coat-hangered garments over your arm and so exhausted from fighting off assaults by the lazy but avid who have not had the enterprise to pick out a gaggle of garments for themselves, but keep preying upon yours and attempting to pluck them in front of your very eyes from the rack you have preempted to make your selections from, that you go home literally reeling.

"Just looking," say the hands that are fondling your garments, pulling them hither and yon and jerking the dress off the coat-hanger as they hunt for the price-tag. "I'm not taking it away, am I? I can just *look,* can't I? What's that, a size twelve? You sure you're taking it? . . . just let me hold it up again to see how the belt goes."

I have seen customers, veterans of an all-morning sale, wandering about in punch-drunk fashion, forgetting what they had originally come in for, or even where the stairs that lead to fresh air and freedom are. Everybody looks at them sympathetically.

We aficionados of Filene's B.B. understand well their plight.

BEACON HILL: *Hub of the Universe*

A BOSTON CHAMPION

No Victorian lily she. . .

A BOSTON CHAMPION

Up the hill from me a way, I have a neighbor who is something of a local celebrity. She was, at one time, something of an international one; a great sportswoman in a day when croquet was considered a rough game for ladies. She was one of that rare breed of Amazon who surfaced about the time of Woman Suffrage. Their pictures may still be seen in any collection of yellowed photographs — straight-backed, strong-jawed young women, neatly white-collared beneath their formidable chins, with a heft to back up the look in their eyes that said, "I can lick any two men single-handed."

Understandably, few of this Amazon breed wed; they must have been down-right terrifying to the Victorian gentleman still dreaming of the lily-like Victorian lady, with her hourglass waist and her propensity for swooning on all appropriate occasions. These strong-chinned young women served, none the less, as the Wave of the Future; leaving the croquet mallet rotting unused on the lawns of their parents, they went out and fired the golf shots heard round the world.

Preeminent in this breed, and like the others unwed, was my neighbor; she and her sister knocked down all the trophies available in this country and moved on to England, that sportswoman's Paradise, where they bowled over all the awards offered there; for they were an unstoppable breed.

One of a large family, my neighbor in her old family house (in front of which, aged 90-plus, she may often be seen vigorously shoveling snow in inclement weather) is now the last one lingering on the vine. Vine-lingering is not exactly her dish, however; and it is only the lifelong care of her devoted Irish staff that keeps her from breaking her neck in bad weather by stomping about the Hill as she has always been accustomed.

A friend told me of the vain attempts made to stop her from going out in blizzards by her household. Dropping by one day on her way to mail a small package, in a blinding snowstorm, at the State House post office, she found Miss Bangs sallying forth, wrapped and booted, with her whole staff fighting a last-ditch delaying action at the door.

Appealed to "to stop Miss Bangs from going out in this storm and getting her death," she attempted to take a firm hand.

"This is nonsense, Lillian — there is a bad blizzard raging, the streets are slippery and you are very likely to break a leg. Let me take your package for you — I'm on the way to the post office anyway."

Balked of her intention, Miss Bangs demurred. It wasn't far to the post office. She was prepared to go. She needed a walk. Liverish. Anyway, the package wasn't wrapped yet.

"I'll wrap it."

Miss Bangs put up a less strenuous objection to this — because, she was forced to admit, she disliked wrapping packages. This was, however, a Christmas present to her niece's family. It must go today.

It turned out to be a big bundle of odd-sized gloves from the nether regions of Filene's. Miss Bangs never remembers people's individual sizes and she doesn't try; she simply goes to some store where she observes a sale in progress, and buys six pairs of assorted sizes for a family of six. It is her theory that that way, something is bound to turn up to fit everybody. They can shuffle them out for themselves on arrival.

My friend went to Miss Bangs' desk where she encountered hundreds of rounds of carefully tied-up string, old Revere bowls full of chewed-up pencils and erasers, and eventually, a large manila envelope into which she stuffed the assorted gloves.

"Oh, you can't have that!" Miss Bangs protested.

"Why not? It's big enough."

"But," Miss Bangs said, shocked, "it hasn't been *used*!"

A large luncheon, on her 90th birthday, was given for her at a neighboring woman's club, both to celebrate the occasion and to voice, before a large and admiring company of ladies, her many accomplishments.

It could early be perceived that Miss Bangs' achievements had been parcelled out among the various lady speakers, to be dwelt on one at a time. This one recounted her early Civic endeavors, that one her role in golf, this one the records she had broken in tennis, etc.

The indulgent and admiring ladies who surrounded her applauded each new saga warmly, with increasing interest.

Not so Miss Bangs. As the last speaker rose to salute her, she seized the rose-colored jacket of the lady speaker and gave it a hearty jerk. As the lady bent deferentially towards her Miss Bangs, in a throaty bark which carried easily beyond the first twenty rows, muttered hoarsely, "Cut it *short,* will you?"

BEACON HILL: *Hub of the Universe*

BOSTON HATS

Styles may come and go, but a Boston hat endures forever

Boston hats are, of course, deservedly famous, as is the reply of the lady asked by an awed observer where she bought hers.

"Where do I buy my hats? Oh, we don't *buy* our hats — we *have* our hats."

A look at a good dressy winter hat on a Boston woman induces the thought that they are indeed worth preserving — built for long wear, like the mohair sofa and the horsehair armchairs in the livingroom — not to be lightly discarded like the flimsier transient whimsies of New York. To the slightly irreverent eye of an outsider to Boston Mores, it looks as if Boston hats were selected first for mileage — so many yards of good stout felt, then for decoration — how many loops of purple and cherry-colored velvet is there room for on the crown of the hat? And lastly for Eminence — can the lady in back of you, when you are seated, see any portion of the lecturer in the front of the room? If so, the hat is a failure.

It is only fair to add that nowadays, at Symphony, the younger generation at least is generally hatless or with the flattest of veiled creations, in deference to the row of ladies in back — who, it may also be remarked, would not hesitate to ask a visiting queen to remove her hat should it interfere with their unobstructed view of the second violinist.

I remember once walking the wide sidewalks of Fifty-Seventh Street, in New York City and suddenly seeing in front of me three hats whose lofty silhouettes were so imposingly familiar, so stately and out-of-place on the modern skyline, that I said to myself, "If I didn't know they were safely bedded down in Boston, I'd say those hats *must* belong to my husband's aunts."

I came abreast, and discovered that the hats did indeed belong to my husband's aunts.

They were making their annual sacrificial visit to an old friend who happened to live, unfortunately, in New York.

An illustration of how integral a part of her a good Boston hat can be to a Boston lady, is shown by a story told me by an acquaintance recently.

"Did you ever know Eleanor Atherton?" she said, mentioning a well-known Grande Dame of Boston. "No? Well if you knew her you'd know that she swears like a Duchess, or a trooper, whichever you prefer. Last year, when I was working for some very high-toned charities indeed, I went to a meeting in Chestnut Hill on Conservation. I had had a very rushed day and was aware that my coiffure wasn't up to scratch, but I had a rather pretty hat covering most of my hair, so I didn't worry.

"When I got there I found a great crowd of women already assembled and as I was going upstairs to take off my wrap my hostess said to me, 'We are asking *everyone* to take off her hat, because the Governor's wife is here and we are going to take a big group picture, so everyone must be hatless.'

"Well, I knew my hair to be more like a bird's nest than anything else at this point, so I grumbled and fussed for a while, did the best I could with my fingers to my messy hair, and went downstairs.

"There the first person I saw, in the middle of the room, was Eleanor Atherton, sitting there in a hat that *was* a hat. I mean to say it was August, and rather hot, muggy weather, but she had on her head a sort of great big heavy bonbon of dark-brown felt that hugged her head tightly and seemed, beside, to spread out all around her.

"I went up to her and said, 'Well, this is what I call favoritism. Here they make me take off my hat and *you* sit there with that great big hat on.'

" 'Oh, I couldn't be bothered with all that damned nonsense,' she said in her deep, booming voice. 'But you know what happened to me yesterday? I'd had a really very exhausting day from beginning to end — shopping, luncheon engagement, appointment here, appointment there. By the time I got home late in the day I was worn out. I was too tired to go down to dinner so I said to myself, I'll just get in a nice hot tub and have a good long soak, and have a tray sent up to my room so I can tumble in bed and get a good night's sleep.

" 'And that's what I did. Only, in spite of being so tired, I couldn't seem to get to sleep. I tossed and I turned and I lay this way and that, but I just couldn't seem to relax and get comfortable. Finally, I put my hands up to my head and you know what was bothering me? It was that God-damned hat.' "

BEACON HILL: *Hub of the Universe*

BOSTON TOURS

From the Freedom Trail to your neighbor's bedrooms — a tour for every fancy

Boston does not have the Grand Canyon, nor boiling mud springs nor two-story waterfalls on view. Nevertheless, it is a great place for tours.

What we have on display is History.

If you come right down to it, every place in the country has history. But the ruts made by Covered Wagons bumping across the Great Plains have long since faded; the many areas where hard-pressed frontiersmen, their scalps intact, bounded into stockades two jumps ahead of pursuing Indians are unrecorded; there are no marks to show the rivers forded, the forests cut down.

It is in stone and brick, the little shells man has built to cover his frailty, that history can most easily be shown. In Boston, these remain. Faneuil Hall, that knew the steps of Samuel Adams, Ben Franklin, John Hancock, is still here. The Old State House, Bunker Hill with its monument, Old Ironsides at its dock, Paul Revere's house — all these are here to be seen. The blue tourist buses roll daily by Shem Drowne's weathervane of the golden grasshopper, swinging above the marketplace in the east wind.

In no time flat we found ourselves out in the backyard with trowels in our hands and a big bucket of mortar.

Beside these formal historical tours, there are other tours, on foot, to be made. You can, of course, follow the Freedom Trail marked out in red brick, and walk through the Italian North End district, where old men sit about in groups on the street, where marvelous fruit and vegetable stalls bursting with color and ripeness beguile the eye, where flaky pastries and crusty fresh Italian bread are temptingly set out, where white-furred rabbits hang on meat hooks in the butchers' windows. Or you may visit the Old North Church, where Paul Revere's friend set "two lanterns aloft," and frustrated the hard-rowing English.

But for those with a real yen for the aching foot, there are House Tours and Garden Tours.

House Tours are usually the most expensive, whether with an unconscious bow to the hostess who has knocked herself cold before this event striving to give the effect of Splendid and Effortless Living, or because the wear and tear on the furniture has to be thought of. Nevertheless they are extremely popular.

I can't help feeling that part at least of this popularity is caused by the indisputable New England passion to get upstairs in a neighbor's house and Nose About. I don't mean necessarily in an unfriendly way; I just mean Nose About. I can't help the suspicion that New England housewives have a special fondness for getting behind the formal facade of a neighbor — the parlor set in state, the downstairs hall — and seeing What Goes On Behind the Scenes, as it were.

The first time I was signed up for Community Chest calls in a New England town, I remember the outrage in our Chairman's voice as she said to me, "What, she *took you upstairs*? In all the years I've known her, that woman has never let me upstairs in her house!"

Whether for this or other reasons, the number of people who pay their money to take these tours is really astonishing. They come from all over the world; from India, Scotland, South America, Norway, and from every city and town in the United States. They come in wheelchairs, on crutches, with babies strapped on their backs or with old ladies who are hauled, panting, up and down the steps. While women, of course, outnumber men, the masculine sex is well represented by young artists, architects, and elderly connoisseurs of china, glass or gardens. In fact a large percentage of the visitors are more knowledgeable about the objects they are viewing than the hostess who is showing them, who may just have inherited her unusual old pieces.

Long before the opening hour of ten, a line will have been forming in the street composed of those true zealots who prefer to get there early and observe what they have come to observe before the larger crowds obstruct the view. When the doors are flung open, and the lady who sits behind the table at the door begins taking tickets and tallying numbers in her little book, splendor is revealed; the furniture shining, the flowers carefully arranged, every cushion on the sofa in artfully-placed order.

But O, had someone accidentally thrown open the doors half an hour before!

Nobody who has not been through the ordeal of a house-showing can have any idea of what last-minute panic prevails. The large packet of clothes from the dry cleaners, expected vainly for weeks, which arrives suddenly and has to be paid for then and there; the pot of ivy someone manages to break all over the front hall, scattering dirt and leaves over carpet and staircase just before the door is opened; the "hostesses", necessary guides and caretakers, who arrive late or never; the gate to the garden which jams, the discovery that the lady next door has chosen this time to set out conspicuously her three overflowing garbage pails; that the change for the ticket-buyers has not come, and the notebook for listing the number of guests is mysteriously missing; all these are merely Par for the Course.

Not long after my arrival in Boston pressure was brought on me to Show My Garden.

The only trouble was, I didn't have any. I pointed this out, with some diffidence. In back of our old brick house was the usual small back yard paved with brick, and a giant weed-tree, or ailanthus, thrusting up in a corner.

No matter, said the iron-willed powers who were arranging a garden tour. You can make one.

Had I known what this entailed, I would have taken the first plane out for Africa. But skilled prevaricators that they were, they made it sound so easy. You simply get a bricklayer to put up two-foot terraces around the yard, fill with earth and plant with flowers. Simple, isn't it?

In no time flat we found ourselves out in the back yard on our hands and knees with trowels in our hands and a big bucket of mortar.

An estimate from the bricklayer had done it. My husband can drag his feet skillfully for weeks over some project I am enthusiastically pursuing; but let him get an outside estimate of the cost, and he's out and at work like something shot from a gun.

We learned the bricklayer's trade fast. We had plenty of old brick, from the material we had had to pull up to make the flower beds. We broke bricks in two with the trowel, and made beautiful curves. Every time our knees gave out or our hands lost too much skin, we thought of the estimate and were filled with new zest.

We even had a little wall fountain in place by spring. (Another estimate had done it.) "Five hundred dollars?" my husband shouted. "Gimme that hammer."

I hadn't realized, though, how early the press had to be admitted for photographs. (To whet interest, photographs must come out weeks before the actual showing.)

"The inside of the pool isn't painted!" I wailed.

"It's now or never," I was told inexorably. "You let them in or nobody's going to know you *have* a pool."

Ten minutes before the press arrived, I was in dirty dungarees, desperately painting the inside of the pool sky-blue. Ten minutes later, I was posing in my best pink dress by a tree. (Supposedly, this was my usual gardening costume.)

But I was humiliated to see that the blue paint had come off, and was floating in big gobs on the surface of the pool.

And I painted the back stairs, leading to the garden passageway, too late. If we'd had good weather and the white paint had dried, I would never have had to observe the first two ladies walking out the street-level door from the garden with long streaks of white paint on the back of their shoes.

And if I'd instructed my garden hostess more carefully beforehand, a whole bevy of innocent visitors wouldn't have gone out with the wrong name of every shrub in the garden firmly planted in their heads.

And if the weather hadn't been almost as malicious about gardens as it is about beaux arts, I wouldn't have broken the drought.

It would have been smarter to have taken that plane to Africa.

BEACON HILL: *Hub of the Universe*

CRIME ON BEACON HILL

Where personality runs rampant, crime doesn't always pay

It was not to be expected that, with crime rampant everywhere in cities, Beacon Hill would be spared. But, typically, Beacon Hill has met crime in its own individual way.

Even the burglars have adopted their own particular style for Beacon Hill. There was, for example, the gentleman who became famous overnight as The Beacon Hill Burglar. His method of robbing a house (which he plied up and down Chestnut and Mt. Vernon Streets with considerable success) was to punch in the long glass panels which run, in old Beacon Hill houses, on either side of the front door. He would then reach in a hand, turn the lock in the door, and let himself in with no trouble at all.

Up and down the Hill, sympathy was in order whenever one observed a smashed pane by the front door. The local glass cutter enjoyed a bumper crop of business.

The people next door to us were robbed, and it led to a considerable estrangement between them and their Great Dane — a large and impressive-looking animal who had, far from attacking the intruder, ap-

"They've dashed by the frog pond — but those other two are gaining on them!"

parently welcomed him in — delighted to have company while his owners were away.

The police, with their rather obvious minds, began looking for a gentleman with a bandaged right hand. Meeting such a one on Mt. Vernon Street one fine morning, they politely invited him into their squad car with them, and the Side-Panel Robberies on Beacon Hill came to an abrupt stop.

Crime, however, had by no means left the Hill. Even cream, it was discovered, could no longer be left on the doorstep. The Hood milkman, clanking about like the chatelaine of a medieval castle by the dawn's early light, was compelled to carry a large bunch of keys at his belt — at least a pound's worth — with which to unlock the front doors of his individual customers, set the cream down inside, and lock up after himself. Bronze Historical Markers on Beacon Hill monuments and houses alike disappeared, the booty of a new type of Collector. One morning a whole block's heavy copper drainpipes were found to be Gone With The Wind.

Persons who have had their houses Broken and Entered more than once often go to the considerable expense of having their homes burglarproofed with an expensive alarm system which will, presumably, bring the police to their house on the dead run. Unfortunately, they are much more likely to set it off themselves. No subsequent telephone call explaining what has happened will call off the police; the call, they say, might have been put in by the burglar, to throw them off. One woman complains that her terrier has been setting off the alarm on purpose.

"He does it *deliberately* . He likes the excitement, and he's learned how to trigger it."

Others have taken refuge in heavy decorative ironwork grills, over windows and doors, to be locked every night. Only trouble is, one must be careful with the keys; should they be mislaid, and the house catch fire, one could be cooked to a fine turn before the keys ever turned up.

Then there was the gentleman who inadvertently arranged deluxe summer accommodations for the passing stranger who happened to see his key left carelessly sitting in the lock. This happened in the winter, and the stranger did nothing about it while the family was in residence; but cannily waited till summer when they were away, and let himself in (by his own later confession) every weekend, used their bathroom facilities to bathe in, their mirrors to shave in, their amply-supplied kitchen for meals; and, last but not least, emptied their wall safe of its contents.

Most of the antique shops, even the lovely candy shop on Charles Street are now kept locked; the shopper has to ring a bell and submit to a sharp scrutiny before being admitted. Tenants in some of the more expensive apartment houses have banded together to keep the outer lobby door locked at all times; it leads to considerable difficulty about deliveries.

Worst of all were the muggings and purse snatchings. Meetings by the Beacon Hill Civic Association and others were hastily convened. The fact that Beacon Hill is dimly and artistically lit by a few sparsely-placed street lights, and many of the inhabitants elderly and not exactly geared for track practice, contributed to the general problem. Committees of vigilantes were proposed, but turned down on the civilized grounds that such self-appointed arbiters of Law and Order are liable to get out of hand, and need policing themselves.

At last a partial solution was found; everybody was instructed to buy a large police whistle, sold at a certain popular hardware store on The Hill, and blow this fiercely in the face of an attack. Presumably, help either from the police or from neighboring citizens would be at once forthcoming.

Never mind the cynic who was heard to say that he found it more helpful to yell, 'Fire!' "You may be left bloody and unconscious in the street after an attack," he said, "by persons more anxious to get away than to assist you; but 'Fire!' insures that a large curious crowd will rush to your vicinity at once."

Almost everyone on the Hill has a large whistle now, and once or twice it has actually brought help. But another solution was recently found by two ladies who live in my vicinity. Walking quietly home up Walnut Street after the Friday afternoon symphony, they encountered two skylarking youths who zigzagged towards them. The shorter youth bowed courteously and greeted one of the pair. As he did, he twisted her bag skillfully from her hand and raced, with his companion, towards the Common. (All handbag thieves make at once for the Common.)

But these two ladies were made of sturdy stuff. No imitation police whistles for them. One of them, after a loud and finely-executed Hollywood-style scream when her bag was seized, made for the center of the street and shouted, "STOP THIEF!" The other took off after the thieves, now racing up Beacon Street, bawling at the top of her lungs, "STOP THIEF!"

It was a slightly old-fashioned form of address, she had to admit, taxed with it later. Nowadays, for one thing, nobody is called a thief; they have simply, "borrowed a car without the owner's permission," "swiped," "liberated," or performed a "ripoff."

Nevertheless, she says, everybody knew what she meant. She pounded up Beacon Street after the two fleeing youths, shouting as lustily as a slight shortage of breath would permit. As a sudden break in the traffic permitted the pair to dash through to the Common, another youth, standing with a friend at the top of the steps that lead downward thereto, hailed her.

"Did those two grab your bag?"

"Yes. There they go!"

There went the newer two youths, bloodhounds of truth and justice, after them. Having left her glasses at home, she admits she had to rely on the group of friendly spectators who had gathered around her for news of the chase.

"Where are they now?"

"They've dashed by the frog pond. They're taking that slanting shortcut to Boylston Street. But those other two are gaining on them."

Sure enough, in about two minutes the good Samaritans came back smilingly swinging her bag by its handles — and wouldn't accept a reward, wouldn't even give their names to the grateful ladies. "They chucked the bag when they saw they were going to be caught. Have a nice day now."

And having themselves insured that the ladies would, these anonymous angels went their way, leaving a crowd stunned by the unaccustomed impact of good news.

Asked later if she couldn't have done as well with one of the Beacon Hill police whistles, the lady answered spiritedly.

"Certainly not! Who'd have turned a hair if I'd blown a whistle? It was the personal touch that did it."

She may be right.

BEACON HILL: *Hub of the Universe*

COLD ROAST BOSTON: ABIGAIL

Just as certain cities capture the character of a country, so certain individuals personify a city...

Before I ever got to Boston, I had heard the term, "Cold Roast Boston." But until I met Abigail, I don't think I really knew what it meant.

Just as certain cities manage to capture, on a smaller scale, the whole character of a country, so certain individuals somehow personify, in themselves, the flavor of a city; and would be, one feels, as completely out of place somewhere else as a cauliflower in a rose bed.

Such a character is my connection-by-marriage, Abigail. If I met Abigail riding a camel in the midst of the Gobi desert, I would still know instantly that she came from Boston; and would be sure her first words would be a statement as to how soon she was going to be able to return to that desirable spot.

Many things about the present day are highly upsetting to Abigail. Her way of coping with them is to ignore them; pretend, as well as she can, that they don't exist. The increasing traffic in the streets is frightening to her, constituting a distinct hazard in combination with her own increasing weight, so that she finds it difficult to safely cross a street in the short and variable space between changing lights. She has been known to walk to the end of a block for the purpose of descending the stairs at a subway station, crossing the tunnel underground, and surfacing, out-of-breath but intact, like a large tweed-covered mole, on the other side of the street.

Looking the epitome of Boston as she does, she is constantly hailed by out-of-town visitors for directions as to how to get about the streets. Abigail can give these, of course; she is familiar with the twists and turns of every smallest alleyway in Boston; but she makes the visitors pay for the information.

"If you are really strangers here," says Abigail in her clear, clipped accents, "I should think the first thing you would do would be to get yourselves a good map of Boston. I cannot *imagine* how you think you can get around Boston without one. Now, if I were visiting *your* city . . ."

Her way of dealing with wrong telephone numbers is likewise admirably constructive. Unlike the rest of us who are inclined to deal with the matter on a superficial level and brush the caller off the line as quickly as possible, Abigail, typically, probes the subject more deeply.

"What made you think you *had* the right number?" Abigail demands. "Did you just look it up in the telephone book and then try and keep the number in your head?"

Yes, the caller admits, he did just that. In fact, what other way is there?

"You should have written the number down, at once, on a piece of paper," Abigail says. "If you had written it down, and had it there to look at, right in front of you, you wouldn't have made this silly mistake, would you? Next time, get out a pencil . . ."

Of course, all the caller has to do is to hang up; he doesn't need to listen to a lecture from Abigail. But there is something authoritative about Abigail's clear stentorian tones, suggesting a female policewoman or, at the very least, a teacher meting out well-merited discipline; callers don't seem to have the nerve to hang up on Abigail.

It is at least safe to assume that Abigail will get very few repeat wrong numbers.

A New England conscience is a magnificent thing for putting iron in the spine. But carried to excess, it can feed, as it were, upon its possessor, making life a torment not only to her but to everyone around her.

Janet, the relative with whom Abigail makes her home, called me in

She has been known to walk to the end of a block, cross the tunnel underground, and surface like a large tweed-covered mole, on the other side of the street.

As his key turned in the lock, the hall light switched on and there was Abigail, sitting up straight in the high-backed chair by the door. . .

distress recently.

"Abigail has been downstairs in the front hall since 5:30 this morning, sitting on that hard little chair, waiting for the postman. It's very exhausting for her. But I can't stop her. She is resolved to catch the postman and give him a thorough dressing down."

From her high eyrie on the floor above, Abigail commands an excellent view of the street; and she makes good use of it. She renders any Substitute Postman's life a perfect Hell. She was able to observe a new postman taking what she considered an unnecessarily circuitous route, up to the farther end of the street and then down, instead of crossing over at the end of the block, which would have gotten Abigail's mail to her ten minutes earlier. When the unfortunate postman rang, she was ready for him.

"I have been watching you," Abigail stated ominously. "Why do you make that silly extra detour instead of bringing the mail straight over the way our regular postman does? You are just wasting time."

The unfortunate postman, taken aback at being accosted furiously in the middle of the morning by an ancient female with blood in her eye, muttered something to the effect that he was doing the best he could.

"No, you are not," said Abigail, who doesn't mind in the least directly contradicting anyone with whom she happens to disagree. "That is just what you are *not* doing. That is why I have been sitting here since 5:30 this morning waiting to speak to you about it. The other postman *never* takes the route you did."

The young postman said feebly, "Well, I guess everyone has a different way of doing things, don't they?"

"No they do not," said Abigail, not accepting this argument for a second. (Indeed, Abigail never accepts anyone else's argument.) "If they are interested in doing things the right way, there is only one right way to do it. And you happen to be doing it the *wrong* way. Now, if you would like me to tell you the *right* way . . ."

The young postman now crosses over, as directed by Abigail, at the end of the block. He slinks across rather furtively, as one conscious that unseen eyes are upon him; and doesn't look fully relaxed until he gets to the next street.

Having, one day, just missed her at her house with an important message, I was lucky enough to perceive her, large in purple tweed, moving like the noontime shadow of a rock along the other side of Charles Street. Anxious to catch her before she moved out of my ken, I stepped lightly between two half-ton trucks and in front of a careening taxi to gain the other side and deliver the message to a startled Abigail.

Abigail was not grateful. Staring at me wrathfully, bristling with outraged disapproval, she said coldly, making every clipped syllable count, "I do not approve of jaywalking."

I waved jauntily (I am used to Abigail) and made my way back across the street. Above the angry honking of horns and screaming of brakes, I heard Abigail's words — drawn from her reluctantly, but with the obvious compulsion of the Boston Brahmin to give credit where credit is due.

"But thank you, anyway," said Abigail.

When Janet, the relative with whom Abigail makes her home, was temporarily confined to a hospital, my husband was commissioned to check the house and, incidentally, Abigail.

As his key turned in the lock, the hall light switched on and there was Abigail, sitting up straight in the high-backed chair by the door. Before he could ask her what she was doing there, she had shot the same question at him.

"Janet asked me to," my husband explained. "She wanted me to just go through the house and see how you are."

"Well, what does she want me to do?"

"Nothing, nothing!" my husband said hastily. "She just wanted me to make sure you were all right — hadn't fallen downstairs or anything."

"I have no intention of falling downstairs."

"And Janet wanted to know if you were reading about that swindle they're writing up in the newspapers."

"No I am not," Abigail said tartly. "Janet keeps wanting me to read that and form an opinion. But I am not going to. I know nothing about these people. Why should I form an opinion?"

"Oh well, it's just interesting to read and speculate about, you know. Like wondering how a horse race will come out."

"I don't approve of horse racing. And I have no interest in knowing how a horse race will come out."

I in turn received my comeuppance when I called, at Janet's behest, to invite Abigail to dinner.

"No, thank you," said Abigail. "It's very kind of you, but I feel I should stay here where I can watch over the house."

"Oh, come on, Abigail! Just for an hour or so. It will do you good."

"I am *not ill* !" said Abigail furiously, "and I don't need to be done good to!"

Then, suddenly realizing that she had not only mixed up her grammar a bit but was not being very polite, she added hastily, "Thank you. It's very kind of you. But I don't want to leave the house."

"Have you got some good books?"

"Yes, I like to read in bed. I often read the dictionary; dictionaries are very fascinating to read. I am at present going through the Penguin Paperback."

"Do you find it enlarges your vocabulary?"

"I don't know that it enlarges my vocabulary. But it's very fascinating the way it tells you to pronounce certain words. I often don't agree with them *at all* ."

The thought of Abigail nightly pummelling, in absentia, an unknown dictionary opponent, was a little unsettling. Thinking to divert her, or at least change the subject, "Have you ever been to Spain, Abigail?" I asked.

"No, I have not. Why should I go to Spain? I never travelled anywhere without a good reason, and I had no good reason to go to Spain. Now it was necessary that I go to Danzig, so I *went* to Danzig."

I became aware that I had had all the argument I needed for one day, and rose to go home. It was then that Abigail conferred on me her finishing statement of the day, whether in apology or boast I could not say.

"At times," said Abigail, "I allow myself to be extremely disagreeable. I haven't much time left to be disagreeable *in* , so I might as well enjoy doing it while I can."

BEACON HILL: *Hub of the Universe*

CHRISTMAS EVE ON BEACON HILL

Where else would you be expected to have your presents wrapped, tree trimmed, and house decorated by five o'clock on Christmas Eve . . .

CHRISTMAS EVE ON BEACON HILL 

Perhaps no other day of the year is as celebrated, far and wide, as Christmas Eve on Beacon Hill in Boston.

Candles in the windows! Snow on the ground! Carollers trilling carols up and down The Hill in front of the lighted windows! Bell ringers handbell-ringing the ancient tunes! Gay crowds streaming from lighted doorways! Open House everywhere with brimming bowls of froth-coated eggnog, silver salvers holding paper-thin sandwiches, cookies, delicious slices of rich dark fruitcake, everywhere dispensed — Hospitality unbounded. The Hill At Home to the world!

Well, that's the way they tell me it was, anyway. Of late years the fine quality of Beacon Hill hospitality has distinctly dimmed.

Anyone slightly unsteady on his pins is likely to be knocked down and trampled on by the crowds now surging over The Hill, whose acquaintance with the old carols is apt to be limited to the first verse of Silent Night belted out on a Salvation Army trumpet. Inhabitants of Beacon Hill houses show an increasing disinclination to giving out news of their impending At Homes, for fear of what might drop in on them. Candles in the windows are electric, or there are lamps dimly seen through tight-pulled shades.

I do not know (though, like every other happening on The Hill, it is undoubtedly faithfully chronicled somewhere) who lit the first candle in a window on Beacon Hill on Christmas Eve. But I could shoot him. Where else but in Boston would you be expected to have all your chores done, your presents wrapped, your tree trimmed, your wreaths neatly up in place and your house suitably decorated, by five o'clock on Christmas Eve, so that you could spend the evening wandering Beacon Hill in carefree fashion, slurping up eggnog as you went?

And what eggnog. I do not want to seem critical, but every hostess on Beacon Hill has a different idea of what constitutes a good eggnog. Hood's standard mixture, bought from the milk company by the quart, usually predominates and is probably the safest brew if one is accepting much hospitality; but the endless variations played on this basic recipe constitute a challenge to the strongest stomach. As to what is contained in

"We must never," I said to my husband as we sprawled, exhausted, on the sofa, "do this again." .

the various wine punches offered the unwary guest, that is a secret known only to the individual hostess and her Maker — to whom I trust she is accountable.

I remember one charming hostess asking for my honest opinion of a drink I was trying hard to down with a good countenance. She had, she confided, made it herself.

When someone first tells you she has made something herself, and then asks you for your honest opinion of it, even the dullest-witted can sense that anything but an honest opinion is called for. I told my hostess her punch was delicious, inwardly praying that I might not be smitten dead for such a horrendous lie.

"O I'm so glad," she said. "You see the wine we usually put in it didn't come, so I improvised. I used half a bottle of cooking sherry, and the rest of some brandy we had on the kitchen shelf — anyway I *think* it was brandy — and then I tossed in a couple of different wines, just to give it more *flavor*, you know. I do think it has a distinctive flavor, don't you?"

It did.

Then there are those who go in for what they inform you is Swedish Glögg. Swedish Glögg, so far as an impartial observer can note, is a combination of anything spirituous your host happens to have on his shelf, combined with every spice in the kitchen cabinet. I first encountered Swedish Glögg three-quarters of the way up The Hill on our first Christmas Eve there, and I was devoutly thankful that I was almost home. For three or four days thereafter I was chained to the cold-water faucet, trying vainly to slake an unquenchable thirst. After this I became more knowledgeable about whose hospitality to sample lightly.

But I have never become very apt at Beacon Hill Christmas Eves. Granted a chronic inefficiency on my part which never allows me to have all my Christmas chores done by the time dusk descends on Beacon Hill, I still cannot consider the institution a sound one.

There is the basic problem of ill-assorted guests. All ages are encouraged to mingle at Beacon Hill Open Houses, and a charming idea it is too, viewed impartially. But how do you insure in your guests the kind of saving radar-instinct so highly developed in bats, to enable the obviously uncongenial and ill-assorted to avoid one another? The hours for Open House are loose — roughly from six to ten o'clock. This gives four hours in which every conceivable social disaster can take place.

Never shall I forget the first year we timidly decided, after a particularly disastrous bout the year before with eggnog and Glögg, to be At Home ourselves.

When At Home on The Hill, you make yourself deliberately vulnerable — light all the lights, have the windows glowing and the door ajar, fill up the brimming bowl, and wait.

Nothing happens. Nothing continues to happen. If you are not careful, you begin to nervously drink up the eggnog yourself. This can be disastrous.

At about nine o'clock that night we had had two cups of eggnog apiece and had exhausted all the small talk possible between a man and his wife who have been exchanging conversation for almost twenty years.

Then suddenly the doorbell pealed — first one loud cheerful ring and then another. Two sets of guests at once! We leaped to our feet.

Through the doorway came the most elderly and formal couple of our acquaintance — a retired General of the Ancien Régime and his beautiful but distinctly reserved lady. They were closely followed by a drunken stockbroker, whom my husband had up to now seen only in his office, and a lady whom he jovially introduced as his New Girl Friend.

Ours was all-too-obviously not the first hospitality they had sampled that night. "We're doing The Hill," our caller explained jovially, "and saw your light on." I said to Myrtle here, "Thass where the Howards live and we're gonna go in and wish them a Merry Christmas."

They have not been back since; but neither have the General and his lady.

This encounter set the pace for the entire evening. A swinging bachelor, pausing on his way to larger and giddier gatherings below us on The Hill, was paired with a young couple from the Outermost Suburbs with a wallet full of pictures of their new baby which they whipped out as they came through the doorway. Two sisters-in-law famous for not being on speaking terms with each other met in our living room. The minister and his wife, dutifully calling on us as new parishioners, were coupled with an elderly man-about-town famous for his racy stories. At one time we had a clutch of six old ladies in search of giddier fare, none of them at all pleased to meet.

In between these extraordinarily unfortunate encounters, there would be arid stretches when the bell did not ring, in which there was nothing to do but rinse the dirty eggnog glasses and brace ourselves for the next encounter.

At ten, we threw in the sponge and turned off the lights.

"We must never, never," I said to my husband as we sprawled, exhausted, on the sofa, shoes off and the last of the eggnog rattling in our glasses, "do this again."

Next year we went out. Since a lady below us on The Hill had put "7:30" on her card, we choked down a meal of whatever unappetizing odds and ends could be found in the refrigerator and appeared there first. We found spread out on the festive table a most elaborate buffet supper — delicious cold roast beef, asparagus salad, superb custard-and-cake dessert — everything a starved gourmet could dream of.

"You've *had* dinner already?" our charming hostess trilled as we surveyed this lovely array with glassy eyes. "Oh, but you *shouldn't* have. I thought everyone would know it was dinner by the time I put on the card."

How can you ever know anything by the time a Beacon Hill hostess puts on a card? Hospitality can take any possible form, from a buffet supper to a thimble-size glass of wine. I shall not soon forget an At Home we attended last year.

It was, as Christmas Eves on The Hill are all too likely to be, a spectacularly foul winter night with icy winds of gale force driving buckets of wet snow into the faces of anyone intrepid enough to venture out, slush on the sidewalks with a wicked layer of glaze directly underneath, and small intermittent cloudbursts of hail. It was, in fact, ideal leg-breaking weather, the kind that fills whole wards at Massachusetts General Hospital with traction cases suspended from mobile metal arms. The kind of evening, sentiment notwithstanding, one would prefer to spend bent over a log fire, feeding hunks of hardwood into the roaring flames, the curtains drawn and a hot rum punch at one's elbow.

But a singularly misplaced Samaritan impulse caused me to force my protesting spouse out into the night with me. An old friend who had been away from Boston many years had sent out a rather pathetic bid for us to attend his and his wife's first At Home. Considering the weather, I

But how do you insure in your guests the kind of radar instinct which enables the obviously uncongenial and ill-assorted to avoid one another?

did not think it likely they would have many visitors. As they are the type for whom any form of hospitality means a major effort — they are simply not geared for casual entertaining — and as, besides, they were living high up in a hotel apartment, I felt that someone should show up so that their preparations should not have been in vain.

When the ancient elevator had finally creaked its way to their floor (I send many prayers to the God of Travellers from hoary Boston elevators) we found our friends in hotel-parlored state, surrounded by untasted goodies — elaborate sandwiches, little patisserie-type frosted cookies, thimble-fulls of sherry wine. They greeted us with the warmth people display for visitors who may well be their only guests of the evening, and plied us with wine and little sandwiches.

Our host, however, seemed ill at ease. He was so distrait that I could not help suspecting his wife, a frail lady of hypochondriacal tendencies, was fighting off one of those bouts during which she customarily retires to bed. This was reinforced by snatches of whispered conversation, furtively indulged in, during which I distinctly heard "the doctor" mentioned.

We breathed a sigh of relief as another couple, old friends like ourselves, blew in, covered with snow. Now we could, in good conscience, leave and make a few other scheduled calls.

But our host would not hear of it. "Oh, no, you *mustn't* go till the doctor comes," he said. "We're expecting him any moment — he should have been here by now."

The doctor? We glanced at each other apprehensively. Did our host fear to leave his wife alone? Was there some sort of emergency, gallantly being carried off, we were unaware of?

This impression was further borne out by a hasty and rather surreptitious conversation our host carried on over the bedroom telephone. His voice was lowered, his hand obviously muffling his mouth. As inevitably happens in such cases, only those words carried out to the other room which he would most have preferred to be unheard.

". . . see you shortly, then, . . and don't forget the hypodermic needle."

The hypodermic needle? We settled back apprehensively and reached for our sherry glasses. Obviously a crisis was building up.

Not very long after this, the doorbell pealed again. Our host and hostess brightened visibly. In came a large, jovial professional man accompanied by his wife, son and daughter-in-law. We were all introduced, our host and his wife greeting the new arrivals with a warmth and familiarity obviously accorded more to old friends than to any professional relationship.

The doctor went in to a sort of whispered huddle with our friends, and I caught again the words, "brought the needle."

Waiting for the doctor to take our ailing hostess into the adjoining bedroom and give her whatever emergency treatment she required, I was astonished to see him, instead, steered by our host to an adjoining table. On it was sitting a large, dark, moist chocolate cake. From a lower shelf, our host pulled out a whopping bottle of West Indian rum. The doctor produced from a case in his pocket a long hypodermic needle, filled it from the rum bottle, and in one skilled gesture shot the chocolate cake chock-full of rum.

"There!" said our host, relaxed now and beaming. He rapidly sliced up the cake and put a generous slab on each sandwich plate, handing them round. "Now we can really wish you a Merry Christmas!"